M000308930

DEALING WITH DISASTERS

APPLYING GIS

DEALING

WITH

DISASTERS

GIS FOR EMERGENCY MANAGEMENT

Edited by

Ryan Lanclos
Matt Artz

Esri Press
REDLANDS | CALIFORNIA

Esri Press, 380 New York Street, Redlands, California 92373-8100
Copyright © 2021 Esri
All rights reserved.
Printed in the United States of America
25 24 23 22 21   2 3 4 5 6 7 8 9 10

ISBN: 9781589486393

The information contained in this document is the exclusive property of Esri unless otherwise noted. This work is protected under United States copyright law and the copyright laws of the given countries of origin and applicable international laws, treaties, and/or conventions. No part of this work may be reproduced or transmitted in any form or by any means, electronic or mechanical, including photocopying or recording, or by any information storage or retrieval system, except as expressly permitted in writing by Esri. All requests should be sent to Attention: Contracts and Legal Services Manager, Esri, 380 New York Street, Redlands, California 92373-8100, USA.

The information contained in this document is subject to change without notice.

US Government Restricted/Limited Rights: Any software, documentation, and/or data delivered hereunder is subject to the terms of the License Agreement. The commercial license rights in the License Agreement strictly govern Licensee's use, reproduction, or disclosure of the software, data, and documentation. In no event shall the US Government acquire greater than RESTRICTED/LIMITED RIGHTS. At a minimum, use, duplication, or disclosure by the US Government is subject to restrictions as set forth in FAR §52.227-14 Alternates I, II, and III (DEC 2007); FAR §52.227-19(b) (DEC 2007) and/or FAR §12.211/12.212 (Commercial Technical Data/Computer Software); and DFARS §252.227-7015 (DEC 2011) (Technical Data–Commercial Items) and/or DFARS §227.7202 (Commercial Computer Software and Commercial Computer Software Documentation), as applicable. Contractor/Manufacturer is Esri, 380 New York Street, Redlands, CA 92373-8100, USA.

@esri.com, 3D Analyst, ACORN, Address Coder, ADF, AML, ArcAtlas, ArcCAD, ArcCatalog, ArcCOGO, ArcData, ArcDoc, ArcEdit, ArcEditor, ArcEurope, ArcExplorer, ArcExpress, ArcGIS, ArcGIS CityEngine, arcgis.com, ArcGlobe, ArcGrid, ArcIMS, ARC/INFO, ArcInfo, ArcInfo Librarian, ArcLessons, ArcLocation, ArcLogistics, ArcMap, ArcNetwork, ArcNews, ArcObjects, ArcOpen, ArcPad, ArcPlot, ArcPress, ArcPy, ArcReader, ArcScan, ArcScene, ArcSchool, ArcScripts, ArcSDE, ArcSdl, ArcSketch, ArcStorm, ArcSurvey, ArcTIN, ArcToolbox, ArcTools, ArcUSA, ArcUser, ArcVoyager, ArcWatch, ArcWeb, ArcWorld, ArcXML, Atlas GIS, AtlasWare, Avenue, BAO, Business Analyst, Business Analyst Online, BusinessMAP, CommunityInfo, Database Integrator, DBI Kit, EDN, Esri, esri.com, Esri—Team GIS, Esri—The GIS Company, Esri—The GIS People, Esri—The GIS Software Leader, FormEdit, GeoCollector, Geographic Design System, Geography Matters, Geography Network, geographynetwork.com, Geoloqi, Geotrigger, GIS by Esri, gis.com, GISData Server, GIS Day, gisday.com, GIS for Everyone, JTX, MapIt, Maplex, MapObjects, MapStudio, ModelBuilder, MOLE, MPS—Atlas, PLTS, Rent-a-Tech, SDE, See What Others Can't, SML, Sourcebook·America, SpatiaLABS, Spatial Database Engine, StreetMap, Tapestry, the ARC/INFO logo, the ArcGIS Explorer logo, the ArcGIS logo, the ArcPad logo, the Esri globe logo, the Esri Press logo, The Geographic Advantage, The Geographic Approach, the GIS Day logo, the MapIt logo, The World's Leading Desktop GIS, Water Writes, and Your Personal Geographic Information System are trademarks, service marks, or registered marks of Esri in the United States, the European Community, or certain other jurisdictions. Other companies and products or services mentioned herein may be trademarks, service marks, or registered marks of their respective mark owners.

For purchasing and distribution options (both domestic and international), please visit esripress.esri.com.

On the cover: Photograph by Felix Mittermeier.

CONTENTS

INTRODUCTION

CREATING SAFER, LESS VULNERABLE COMMUNITIES requires a modern approach to understanding threats and hazards that are more complex, costly, and devastating than ever before. Agencies around the world rely on geographic information systems (GIS) every day to plan for and mitigate complex threats and hazards and coordinate response and recovery efforts when disasters and emergencies occur. With the geographic approach, you'll develop a deeper understanding of risk in any situation, and gain real-time data insights for faster, more effective decisions.

Part 1: Disaster preparedness

To effectively plan for, mitigate, and reduce risks, emergency management professionals must incorporate real-time data, big data, and other critical data feeds into their analysis. Data-driven insights help communities effectively prepare for worst-case scenarios. In part 1, we'll explore real-world examples of organizations using GIS for visualizing and analyzing risk, performing real-time analytics, managing mitigation projects, and communicating with the public.

Part 2: Disaster response

Emergency management professionals must become more agile and informed at all points during response efforts. Successfully planning for and responding to growing threats requires agility and effective communication throughout an event. In part 2, we'll look at the ways that GIS tools have been used for robust situational awareness, rapid impact analysis, deploying resources, and communicating with the public.

Part 3: Disaster recovery

Recovery efforts can take years, and it's critical to avoid missteps that delay progress. It's essential to provide emergency management professionals with tools to prioritize work and deliver on every recovery dollar invested in a community. In part 3, we'll see how GIS can be used for better documentation and management of debris removal, distribution of resources, and transparent recovery monitoring.

"Thanks to location technology and the internet, we have never had a better ability to model, measure, and map fast-developing events like hurricanes, tornadoes, earthquakes, fires, or floods. The understanding that comes from this ability allows us to get inside the turning radius of the big challenges we face as a people. So, instead of merely reacting as we chase after a problem, we're actually anticipating and getting ahead of the problem. We are modeling, we are measuring what works, and we are sharing with everyone in real time the latest emerging truth on a map."

—Martin O'Malley, former governor of Maryland, former
mayor of Baltimore, and author of *Smarter Government:
How to Govern for Results in the Information Age* (2019).

HOW TO USE THIS BOOK

THIS BOOK IS DESIGNED TO HELP YOU FOCUS ON ISSUES that matter to you right now. It is a guide for taking first steps with GIS and applying the geographic approach to decisions and operational processes to solve common problems and create a more collaborative environment in your organization. You can use this book to identify where maps, spatial analysis, and GIS apps might be helpful in your work and then, as next steps, learn more about those resources.

Learn about additional GIS resources for emergency management by visiting the web page for this book:

go.esri.com/dwd-resources

PART 1

DISASTER PREPAREDNESS

UNDERSTANDING THE COMPLEX THREATS FACING YOUR community is the first step to planning effective mitigating strategies that reduce risk of loss of life and property. With today's natural disasters and hazards, emergency management professionals can't rely on historical knowledge alone to prepare for tomorrow. GIS maps and analytics allow emergency managers to visualize and analyze potential risks and design proactive mitigation projects that strengthen a community's resilience when disaster strikes.

Locate vulnerable assets and potential hazards

Analyze the risks to citizens and infrastructure. Look for interdependencies you never knew existed. Mapping is an integral step in risk assessment and the foundation for good preparedness.

Prioritize projects to reduce risk and maximize resources

Develop strategies and design programs that target areas and hazards where you can have the greatest impact on reducing loss of life and property while maximizing the resources available.

Use maps to communicate better preparedness

Communicating risks using GIS maps improves readiness, adoption, and success rates of your mitigation plan. Mapping gets everyone on the same page, leading to a more prepared community.

GIS in action

This section will look at real-life stories of how organizations use GIS to prepare for emergencies. The section will also provide you with recommended steps for implementing GIS in your organization.

ENSURING TORNADO WARNINGS WORK WHEN IT MATTERS MOST

Tuscaloosa County Emergency Management Agency, Alabama

I F A NATURAL DISASTER WERE TO STRIKE IN TUSCALOOSA, Alabama, the Tuscaloosa County Emergency Management Agency (TCEMA) would provide leadership, planning, education, and resources to protect lives, property, and the environment. The multi-jurisdictional organization—jointly funded by the City of Tuscaloosa, City of Northport, and Tuscaloosa County—serves all jurisdictions and stakeholders in the county, which is Alabama's second largest by land area. TCEMA also coordinates state and federal resources when any are needed in a disaster management situation.

As part of its disaster preparedness and planning operations, TCEMA maintains outdoor warning sirens throughout the county. These sirens are used to alert the public about tornadoes, which are relatively common in the southeastern United States. As early

The Tuscaloosa County Emergency Management Agency (TCEMA) maintains outdoor warning sirens that alert the public about tornadoes.

warning tools, the sirens are also critical to managing disaster response activities, including mobilizing first responders, coordinating storm shelter needs, and facilitating timely evacuations.

TCEMA needed a way to track not only the siren assets but also its fleet and equipment. To do so, the agency opted to gain location intelligence using ArcGIS along with Esri partner Lucity, Inc.'s Enterprise Asset Management system (Lucity was acquired by CentralSquare in 2019).

Tracking siren inspections in the field

With its tornado siren data strewn across spreadsheets, shapefiles, SDE files, map books, and other paper records, TCEMA was finding it challenging to track the various activities related to doing siren inventories, conducting inspections, performing maintenance, and compiling reports for the Federal Emergency Management Agency (FEMA), because many of the sirens were purchased with federal grant funding. Monitoring these activities was inefficient, time-consuming, and costly—and most importantly, it affected the agency's ability to maintain up-to-date information about the sirens to adequately forewarn citizens of potential danger.

To fix this problem, TCEMA began by making it easier to document inspection and maintenance data. Starting in January 2017, TCEMA identified and validated information about all its sirens in the field. Then, the Tuscaloosa County Public Works (TCPW) department, as a collaborative partner, imported the existing siren shapefile features into its enterprise geodatabase. Finally, Jeannette Byrd, a mapper and GIS analyst at TCPW, set up a web feature service to publish this data to the field via ArcGIS Online. Within approximately three months, TCEMA had a functioning field solution.

Now, using an easily configured ArcGIS Survey123 app that TCEMA built, authorized users from TCEMA and TCPW can

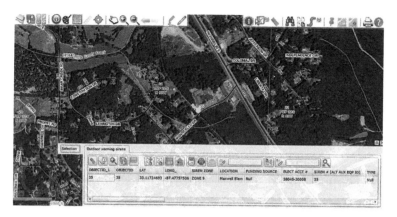

Siren data is now housed in Lucity's Enterprise Asset Management software, which links the GIS features to their related maintenance work orders and cost estimates.

visualize and interact with the siren features in real time. They can record the required attributes for a siren inspection—such as whether the siren is functioning and whether there is vegetation that could interfere with its operation—and simultaneously view and correct each siren's mapped location. With the siren data now housed in Lucity's Enterprise Asset Management software, the GIS features are linked to their related maintenance work orders.

"TCEMA is now able to leverage the Esri platform within and outside the office," said Byrd. "It was simple for us to import the old shapefile of siren locations to our enterprise geodatabase and create the Survey123 application. The app allows the EMA specialists to concurrently record a siren inspection and check the existing mapped location of that siren. The easy picklist format of Survey123 ensures the integrity of the data and a smooth data import into our Lucity asset management system. Tracking work orders in Lucity allows us to document maintenance and, therefore, [reduce] costs."

In addition to optimizing how TCEMA tracks siren inspection and condition data in the field, this real-time process enables the agency to complete its inspection and maintenance reports more quickly and accurately. By giving authorized employees shared access to and visibility of important public service information in ArcGIS—at any time, and from anywhere—TCEMA achieved higher levels of productivity.

"For a project such as this, cost is always a factor," said TCEMA Director Rob Robertson. "The agencies were able to leverage existing Esri and Lucity deployments. Both platforms are flexible, making it easy to adapt our technology investment and increase the [return on investment] of stakeholders' tax dollars."

The data in ArcGIS is also shared with Lucity, TCEMA's system of record for work and maintenance activities. This means the data only has to be updated once before authorized users can have transparent access to the siren data published and shared through ArcGIS. That way, TCEMA and TCPW can easily track and follow up on these required work activities:

- Perform routine maintenance on outdoor warning sirens.

- Ensure that sirens are in proper working condition.

- Maintain regulatory compliance regarding safety and operational readiness.

- Achieve the desired level of disaster preparedness.

"As the outdoor warning sirens age, maintaining these assets becomes more critical," Robertson said. "Having them accurately mapped and tracked means better siren performance and more efficient use of agency funds."

Using ArcGIS Survey 123, EMA specialists can check a siren's location on the agency's existing map at the same time that they conduct a siren inspection.

Optimizing field visits even more

By using the mobile and web capabilities of ArcGIS, TCEMA achieved significant efficiencies in managing its outdoor disaster warning systems. Using focused, mobile apps together with the spatial, interrogative, and analytical functions of ArcGIS Online made it easier for field operations staff to check, fix, and report on critical assets, as well as to coordinate response activities during disaster events.

"The Esri and Lucity platforms are flexible enough to allow us to inspect, maintain, and track county assets not only during routine workflows but also during emergency situations," said Robertson. "Our agencies work together under the Tuscaloosa County umbrella, and now we have a unified system to document and analyze our cooperative efforts."

As part of its ongoing endeavor to further optimize field visits, the agency is looking to use ArcGIS Navigator, which is also integrated with the Lucity work management platform, to help siren inspectors and maintenance workers travel more efficiently to each siren's location. This is expected to strengthen TCEMA's operational foundation and boost workforce productivity, helping the small agency meet its goals more effectively.

"Tuscaloosa County has many remote, rural areas," pointed out Tyler Deierhoi, a GIS and emergency management specialist with TCPW. "Navigation capabilities enable inspection activities to be made efficiently, often when TCEMA staff may be in the area for other types of work. This enables us to not only save on employee hours, but also on fuel costs related to travel."

Deierhoi, along with his colleagues, looks forward to continuing to expand the county's use of GIS and enterprise asset management technology to support additional improvements in emergency management and response across Tuscaloosa County.

This story by Raj Patil originally appeared as "Location intelligence ensures tornado warnings work when it matters most" in the Spring 2018 issue of ArcNews. All images courtesy of Tuscaloosa County Emergency Management Agency unless otherwise noted.

3D MAPPING HELPS PREPARE FOR FLOOD EVENTS

National Science and Technology Center for Disaster Reduction, Taiwan

TAIWAN, A 14,000-SQUARE-MILE ISLAND IN THE PACIFIC Ocean about 100 miles off the coast of China, has a tropical and subtropical climate, which means it is prone to heavy rains and flooding. To help evaluate the viability of flood-based emergency response plans and procedures, the National Science and Technology Center for Disaster Reduction (NCDR) is taking a page out of the military's playbook. Using 3D GIS, the center has put together a war game simulation for flooding.

The Flooding Wargame Simulation Platform for Training and Emergency Response is based on military battle drills, which outline how soldiers will enact specific maneuvers when they encounter certain situations. Applying this concept to flooding is designed to help officials comprehend various disaster situations and determine whether their emergency response plans and procedures—including resources deployment, evacuation support, and route planning for distributing relief supplies—are suitable for reducing the impact of a flood-based disaster. The key to these kinds of drills is to make the simulation as similar to a real disaster as possible.

To do this, NCDR worked with GIS company RiChi Technology and used ArcGIS Enterprise, ArcGIS Pro, and ArcGIS API for JavaScript to build the Flooding Wargame Simulation Platform for Training and Emergency Response. Employing 3D GIS, the platform simulates various types of flooding disasters. Now, officers at emergency operations centers (EOCs) across Taiwan's 22 cities, counties, and special municipalities can use the platform to analyze disaster risk and preparedness when it comes to floods.

An optimized 3D model experience

The research team at NCDR and staff from RiChi Technology built the Flooding Wargame Simulation's 3D GIS platform in two parts. They created the 3D model that processes and displays buildings and, at the same time, integrated that visualization into the platform's functionality.

To build the 3D model, the team used ArcGIS Pro to combine building block shapes with building heights in a feature layer. For the purposes of its technical work, the team published the layer to

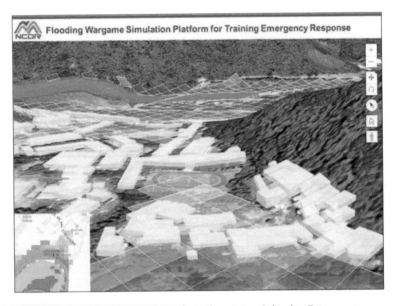

The flood-prone areas around Guishan Elementary School in Taiwan are mapped using the Flooding Wargame Simulation Platform for Training and Emergency Response.

ArcGIS Enterprise and used ArcGIS API for JavaScript to create an app that shows extruded building heights.

To accommodate the lower-performance computers used by some of NCDR's stakeholders, the team implemented a pattern that limits the number of buildings retrieved at one time in the simulation. This helps in more condensed urban environments, for example, by adjusting the model's performance dynamically to each specific flooding simulation. The location of the flood area is set to the center of the map, and the system only displays 3D buildings within a radius of 500 meters from this point. As users pan the map, the 3D buildings form gradually on-screen.

A fast, easy-to-use platform

In designing the platform's functionality, NCDR's primary focus was to make it fast and easy to use. The research team wanted to ensure that the platform could provide analysis results in just a few steps. It also wanted to present those results as thematic maps that show the flood areas, affected populations, any protected objects (for example, vulnerable residents who would need to be escorted out of the flood area), emergency shelters, the network of disaster relief agencies, and a visualization of all this in 3D.

Indeed, the operation contains three steps: users assign a spatial analysis area, set a feasible flooding spot, and enter the flood depth. The system then calculates the lower-elevation areas around the flooding spot to show which locations would likely be affected.

The terrain data comes from a digital terrain model (DTM) with an equally spaced 20-by-20-meter grid. This amount of detail makes efficient computing difficult, though. To reduce the amount of time it takes to calculate what will happen in each section of the grid, the DTM is separated into segments by town. Grids for rivers were omitted from the DTM to reduce the amount of data the platform has to process.

After the flood-prone areas are found, the system computes the different depth levels of the flood in various places by intersecting the lower-elevation areas with impact factors, including which populations and protected objects will be affected. This enables users to see how much of the population will probably need to be rescued. In addition, the system assesses the number of residents that nearby emergency shelters can receive and does a network analysis of rescue resources.

All this information is presented in 2D thematic maps that also show the distribution of emergency and rescue supplies, the locations of large pieces of construction equipment, where disaster relief agencies are located, and more. Commanders from Taiwan's Central Emergency Operations Center (CEOC) and 22 local EOCs can then look at these maps on computers and touch screen monitors to determine the extent of relief services needed and arrange their distribution.

The 3D visualization

Users can also use the Flooding Wargame Simulation Platform to visualize simulated flooding disasters in 3D. This part of the platform is based on the DTM, satellite images, street maps, and the 3D building models. It also integrates real-time video feeds from Taiwan's closed-circuit television (CCTV) monitors. During flood simulation exercises, this helps on-site rescue units communicate and coordinate with each other so they can develop emergency solutions that take into consideration the potential severity of building damage, flooding, and traffic, as well as the viability of potential rescue and escape routes.

Additionally, the platform makes it easier to engage in flood disaster planning for more vulnerable populations. For example, all senior citizen welfare institutions are shown on-screen, and those located on the first floor are marked specifically to take into consideration elderly people who have decreased physical abilities. These details can then help social welfare institutions evaluate their own disaster risk levels and aid other organizations in setting up the

After Typhoon Soudelor struck Taiwan in 2015, Guishan Elementary School was muddy and virtually inaccessible. Satellite imagery shows the school before the disaster (left) and after (right). Photo courtesy of Guishan Elementary School.

government's Prevention and Evacuation Program, arranging emergency housing, and training rescue and response teams.

Being able to take these precautions—and more—in advance of a real flood-based disaster will ensure that Taiwan is well-prepared to weather big storms.

This story by Wen-Ray Su, Chun-Hung Huang, and Chun-Hung Yang originally appeared as "3D GIS helps Taiwan prepare for flood events" in the Winter 2020 issue of ArcNews. All images courtesy of National Science and Technology Center for Disaster Reduction, Taiwan, unless otherwise noted.

COUNTIES ORGANIZE EVACUATIONS WELL IN ADVANCE

US Army Corps of Engineers, New York District

H UNDREDS OF THOUSANDS OF PEOPLE WERE ORDERED TO evacuate before Hurricane Sandy hit the US East Coast in late October 2012. The storm—which reached category 3 status before weakening to a (still powerful) post-tropical cyclone prior to making landfall in New Jersey—became the second-costliest tropical storm in US history.

In Suffolk County, on the eastern part of New York's Long Island, the Office of Emergency Management worked hard to keep residents safe.

"During Sandy, we rescued 250 people from their flooded homes [and] evacuated two major hospitals and several adult homes," said Edward Schneyer, director of emergency preparedness for the Suffolk County Office of Emergency Management.

His colleagues at the agency carried out the rescues effectively because they had storm surge maps created by the US Army Corps of Engineers (USACE), New York District. These maps—which depict where significant amounts of water are likely to get pushed up from the sea and onto land during a tropical storm—help emergency managers in all hurricane-prone states understand the potential extent of storm surges for category 1–4 storms. The maps identify areas where people should evacuate if faced with the threat of a storm surge.

The USACE used ArcGIS Desktop to update these maps with higher-resolution imagery and modeling from the National Hurricane Center's Storm Surge Unit so that agencies can have more accurate information to use when educating the public about how to protect themselves and their property.

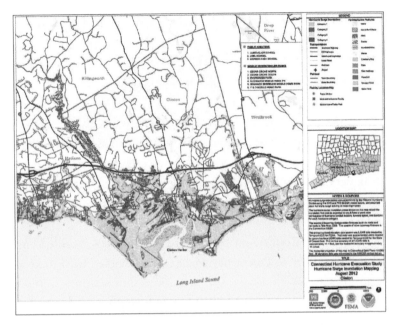

This storm surge map for part of the Connecticut coastline shows the extent of surge for worst-case hurricane landfall scenarios for category 1–4 storms.

Evacuation planning made easier

Developing the storm surge maps is the first step in analyzing hazards for the hurricane evacuation process.

"Historically, 49 percent of human casualties from hurricanes are due to storm surge," said Donald E. Cresitello, USACE Hurricane Evacuation Study program manager for the State of New York. "Other impacts—like riverine flooding due to rainfall, falling trees due to high winds, and indirect impacts like carbon monoxide poisoning and electrocution—can cause deaths [too]."

The federal agency manages hurricane evacuation studies for the National Hurricane Program. The USACE, New York District, is the agency responsible for creating storm surge maps in the New York area as well. To produce the New York Hurricane Evacuation Study Hurricane Surge Inundation Maps, the New York District collaborates with the New England and Baltimore districts of the USACE.

The New York District's storm surge maps go to emergency managers in New York City, Westchester County, and Nassau and Suffolk Counties on Long Island. To help emergency managers learn how to use the maps, the USACE also supplies them in HURREVAC, a decision-making software developed by Sea Island Software for the National Hurricane Program.

Agency officials can use the maps "for evacuation planning [and] to redefine their hurricane evacuation zones, identify where shelters should be located, and identify where assets should be staged prior to impact from a storm," said Cresitello.

"The storm maps serve as a very valuable resource for both government and private sector agencies, as well as private residents," added Schneyer. "As a government agency tasked with emergency management responsibilities pertaining to evacuation and sheltering of the public, we use the maps to gain insight and perspective into the geographical area impacted and use this information to determine the number of buildings or population potentially impacted by a flood."

The Suffolk County Office of Emergency Management can also use the information in the maps to pre-identify damage assessments before a storm even hits the region. This capability is helpful for an area such as Suffolk County, which has approximately 1,000 miles of shoreline and 225,000 residents in its hurricane evacuation zones.

Mapping with new, high-resolution data

To make the higher-resolution storm surge maps, the USACE used ArcGIS Desktop. It took the latest storm surge elevation information from the National Oceanic and Atmospheric Administration's

Hurricane Sandy flooded the Battery Park Underpass, which keeps traffic flowing independently of the labyrinthine streets that make up the southern tip of Manhattan.

(NOAA) SLOSH model (which stands for Sea, Lake, and Overland Surges from Hurricanes) and layered it over high-resolution lidar imagery provided by sources such as the US Geological Survey and offices of emergency management in New York City and New York State. The imagery, which had horizontal resolutions of 0.7 to 2.0 meters, showed the topography of areas in New York that could be affected.

"To come up with the actual depth of water through GIS, we [overlaid] the data out of NOAA's SLOSH model and [subtracted] out the ground elevations using digital elevation models," said Cresitello.

The interagency team working on the project also wrote a Python script to automate tasks such as subtracting the land elevations from the SLOSH model water surface elevations and exporting the maps into PDF files. The team then created maps using ArcGIS Desktop and geodatabase annotation to automatically build a series

The storm surge from Hurricane Sandy flooded Ocean Avenue in Sheepshead Bay, Brooklyn, producing waves on the major thoroughfare. Photo courtesy of JoAnne Castagna.

of layout pages that showed the potential storm surges for the different counties.

Better allocating post-storm resources

The new maps are considerably better than the older ones because the higher-resolution storm surge modeling data and topography are more detailed and accurate. The new maps show the landward extent of inland storm surges and depict the depths of the water (in feet) during different categories of storms. Additionally, the maps illustrate areas that will face more flooding and areas that will experience less.

"Knowing what the depth of water may be in those areas helps emergency managers better perform their initial response after a storm and helps them know what kind of impacts they may expect during these types of storms," said Cresitello.

This knowledge will allow emergency managers to better focus their limited resources as they make critical decisions and lead recovery efforts.

"These storm maps provide the geographical area of primary concern where efforts and resources need to be focused to make essential and accurate damage assessments to determine life and property hazards," said Schneyer. "In the initial stages of a response, our recovery resources are limited—especially for an event the size of Sandy. If resources are dispatched to areas that were not impacted, valuable time is lost mobilizing and reassigning those resources."

Bringing awareness to residents

New York's Hurricane Surge Inundation Areas maps are also for use by the public.

"These maps provide an important level of awareness to residents that either live in a flood area or are preparing to purchase property located in a potential flood zone or hurricane storm surge zone," explained Schneyer.

The ability to see the locations of these zones is why the Suffolk County Office of Emergency Management is bringing this awareness directly to its residents. Agency officials have entered the information from USACE maps into an interactive map on the county's website. Residents can use the web-based map viewer to locate their homes and see if they live in a hurricane storm surge zone. The map displays nearby shelters as well.

The agency also wants the public to use these resources.

The Suffolk County Office of Emergency Management used the storm surge maps to create an interactive web map its residents can use to locate their homes and find nearby shelter locations.

"It's important for people to know their specific zone," said Cresitello. "The public should be aware of what evacuation zone they live in and should listen to their local officials...so they don't question or ignore an official emergency evacuation order."

During Hurricane Sandy, many people who should have evacuated didn't, and they were stranded without help. They faced many dangers, including electrocution from downed power lines and fires from massive gas leaks.

"We don't want the public deciding on their own if they should evacuate or not," continued Cresitello. "If a location is in danger, then they should heed the evacuation order. It doesn't matter if it's six inches or ten feet of water."

"The more information—especially information resulting from scientific studies and available technology—the more situationally aware we and our residents will be," added Schneyer. "This very valuable resource is an excellent tool for public education, emergency management planning, and emergency preparedness in general."

The counties that the USACE, New York District, works with, including Suffolk County, have had access to the maps since 2016.

This story by JoAnne Castagna, EdD, originally appeared as "Counties organize evacuations well in advance" in the Fall 2016 issue of *ArcNews*. All images courtesy of US Army Corps of Engineers, New York District, unless otherwise noted.

DRONE IMAGERY HELPS STAY CRISIS-READY DESPITE GROWTH

North Central Texas Emergency Communications District

W HEN A CALL COMES IN TO 911, ONE OF THE FIRST questions operators ask is, "What's your location?" Because of location privacy concerns, 911 calls cannot always be traced. If the caller doesn't know the exact address of their location, the 911 operator must search for it on a map—referencing nearby landmarks or businesses—before routing emergency services. In areas of new development, the caller's address may not yet appear on the map.

To prevent confusion—and life-threatening delays—staff at 911 call centers strive to keep local maps current. In a fast-expanding region of Texas, North Central Texas Emergency Communications District (NCT9-1-1) updates its maps by using drone imagery and a geographic information system (GIS).

"We've got subdivisions popping up weekly that can each add another 2,000 homes," said Rodger Mann, GIS manager with NCT9-1-1. "There's typically one addressing person in every county and they're overwhelmed by the pace of change."

Aiding with imagery inputs

Across 13 counties surrounding the Dallas-Fort Worth metroplex, NCT9-1-1 serves 42 public safety answering points, each of which dispatches first responders. The service area covers roughly 10,000 square miles, which includes 156 municipalities that are home to 1.6 million people.

One of the counties that NCT9-1-1 serves is Collin County. It includes the fast-growing city of Frisco, which has received many large-business relocations. According to the US Census Bureau, the county grew by 33,753 residents from 2017 to 2018, making it the

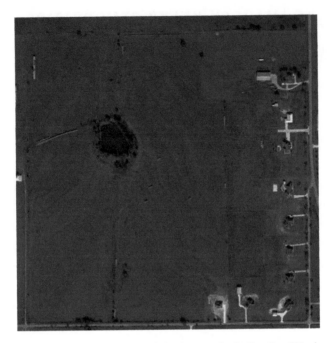

Farm fields are quickly becoming subdivisions in the Dallas-Fort Worth metroplex.

fourth-fastest growing county in the United States. In that same time span, NCT9-1-1 added 15,904 new Collin County addresses—an increase of 7 percent in one year.

To keep up with this growth, NCT9-1-1 partnered with satellite imagery provider Maxar (formerly DigitalGlobe), which provides fresh local imagery every 30 days. NCT9-1-1 also invested in drones to quickly fly and collect imagery for new subdivisions, giving a current picture of what is where.

"We collect and share imagery with addressing authorities to help them speed up the addressing process," Mann said. "We also serve the imagery out in a dispatch environment so that the 9-1-1 telecommunicators can use it to guide first responders and help people in crisis."

Members of the NCT9-1-1 drone crew pause for a picture (left to right, Kasey Cox, David Dean, and Joe Brawner).

With so much growth in their region, the staff members at NCT9-1-1 keep busy.

Flying to the corners of each county

The drone team at NCT9-1-1 consists of four people who work to capture construction as it's being built (pending landowner permission) so that staff in 9-1-1 dispatch centers can see new roads and residences. Up-to-date imagery gives the team peace of mind, knowing, for example, that they're dispatching vehicles to a new subdivision rather than to what would otherwise appear on the map as an open field.

"The drone program has been a dream of ours for two or three years," said David Dean, 911 GIS project coordinator at NCT9-1-1 and lead on the drone program. "Many of our counties purchase new imagery every two years. With our drones, we can fly one day, bring imagery back for processing, and then share it within days."

In addition to capturing new subdivisions, the drones are used to inspect the NCT9-1-1 system of microwave towers that provide a

The Dallas-Fort Worth area continues to grow at a fast pace.

redundant communications network to its fiber and long term evolution (LTE) networks—ensuring that all calls go through.

"Communications outages are a big concern in the 911 community," Mann said. "Fiber cuts do occur pretty often, and they can take out a dispatch center for days. We recently added the microwave network to make sure that kind of thing doesn't happen to any of our counties."

In the interest of providing more precision on the origin of calls, the Federal Communications Commission has been pushing mobile phone carriers to provide z-axis (height) data coming from handsets. NCT9-1-1 is testing the use of drones to create 3D data for tall buildings.

"It's a new concept in public safety to be able to see where someone is calling from within a building," Mann said.

"Thankfully, we live in a digital era where we can do a lot of things remotely and we don't have to travel out to every county," said Bruno Blanco, GIS specialist at NCT9-1-1. "It can take several hours to travel from one end of our NCT9-1-1 region to the other, depending on traffic."

Achieving a shared awareness

NCT9-1-1's ability to collect and share the latest imagery is a fairly recent milestone.

"We had really outdated imagery until recently, and we've long had the need to provide better resolution and more up-to-date inputs for our first responders and 9-1-1 telecommunicators," Mann said. "We just didn't have the staff or expertise to build these datasets and workflows."

NCT9-1-1 worked with Esri to create a semiautomated process using ArcGIS Image Server for gathering imagery inputs and combining them into what is known as mosaic datasets, then publishing imagery services that can be displayed in a variety of applications.

This refreshed imagery helps county addressing personnel and NCT9-1-1 troubleshoot and conduct quality controls on the addresses the agencies receive.

"We've had to go in and align data and details to make them reflect what's on the ground, because our previous imagery wasn't as accurate," Blanco said. "More accurate 911 data eventually leads to better call routing and saves lives."

The team at NCT9-1-1 is careful to document its processes and share essential workflows with other programs.

"That's a nice benefit of doing this work," Mann said. "It doesn't just benefit us—it also benefits our neighbors."

This story by Lawrie Jordan and Ryan Lanclos originally appeared as "How drone imagery helps Texas 9-1-1 agency stay crisis-ready despite growth" on the Esri Blog, October 9, 2019. All images courtesy of North Central Texas Emergency Communications District unless otherwise noted.

SIMULATING A NUCLEAR DISASTER

Lithuanian Fire and Rescue Department

B UILT ABOUT 30 MILES FROM LITHUANIA'S CAPITAL CITY OF Vilnius, the Astravets multireactor nuclear power plant in Belarus is due to begin full operations in 2022, after nearly a decade of construction. The power plant has caused ongoing regional tension and international concern, particularly for Lithuanian government leaders, who consider Astravets a potential risk for a nuclear radiation leak—one that could easily reach a third of Lithuania's 2.8 million people.

Consequently, Lithuania's national leaders instituted civil protection measures. A wide array of federal agency stakeholders participated in this process, including the Fire and Rescue Department (FRD), which is under the Ministry of the Interior; the Government Emergency Commission; subordinate agencies; and other ministries and municipal organizations. Experts at the FRD and the Ministry of the Interior drafted an associated National Emergency Plan for Nuclear Accidents to prepare for the possibility of a nuclear or radiological incident.

In October 2019, Lithuanian government officials directed FRD staff to lead a four-day, multiagency simulation of a nuclear accident. The team needed to thoroughly evaluate its disaster preparedness, response, and recovery procedures to be sure everyone would be ready in the event of a radioactive threat to the Lithuanian people. The objective of this real-world exercise was to put into practice the skills and capabilities of the agencies that comprise the Lithuanian civil protection system by performing the functions defined in the National Emergency Plan for Nuclear Accidents.

"The exercise would allow us to test and practically measure the implementation of functions foreseen in the national plan," said

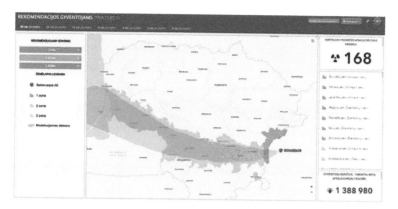

In the event of a nuclear accident at Astravets in Belarus, the Lithuanian government can predict where people will be affected.

Edgaras Geda, head of the civil protection board at FRD. "Preparation and planning for the exercise would be beneficial to participating institutions, enabling them to better understand the complex issues related to a potential radioactive accident at the Belarusian NPP (nuclear power plant). The exercise would also measure interagency cooperation and provide a common understanding of how to carry out the emergency functions."

To perform the emergency simulation effectively, the team needed tools that could help establish a new workflow for the documentation, analysis, and distribution of key operational performance indicators. Esri's local distributor in Lithuania, Hnit-Baltic, introduced FRD to ArcGIS Enterprise, a complete geospatial system that operates behind an organization's firewall or in the cloud, to use for the exercise. The spatial technology included with the platform, such as smart maps, dashboards, and mobile apps, would help stakeholders document, assess, and share safety issues and potential challenges realized during the simulation.

Familiar technology creates a common operating picture

FRD was already familiar with Esri technology. For more than a decade, the department had used earlier versions of ArcGIS, so staff understood that new ArcGIS technology, supplemented with a customized Radiation Incident Module (RIM), could provide a comprehensive process monitoring solution for the emergency exercises.

"With ArcGIS, we would be able to combine spatial data from different sources and provide a real-time common operating picture of the emergency exercises to all involved institutions, shared on smart maps," said Geda. "This was very important for us, not only for the decision-making process within the civil protection system but also for our public information sharing efforts."

The exercise, which aimed to provide a common operating picture to everyone involved, measured interagency cooperation.

For the drill, FRD used the following tools in ArcGIS Enterprise to create a common operating picture for all participants:

- Interactive smart maps informed citizens located within the affected radius of what was happening.

- Thirteen operational dashboards displayed the status of alarm systems, which citizen volunteers had been briefed, the movement of the simulated radiation cloud, the progress of teams collecting data in the field, and more.

- The drill used mobile apps to assign tasks to field personnel who, in turn, used them to record data. These included specialized apps for Lithuania's Environmental Protection Agency and the Radiation Protection Centre.

- ArcGIS StoryMaps provided RIM users with detailed exercise information in a visual format.

During the drill, the Lithuanian government simplified some emergency processes, including how it gathers real-time field data.

Up-to-date, visual information aids decision-making

The simulated nuclear emergency exercise was a rousing success. The team achieved its objective: to measure, improve, and put into practice the skills and capabilities agencies would need if there were a radiation leak at the Astravets nuclear power plant.

"ArcGIS proved to be very useful for the emergency drills, as it provided a single, reliable source of data and information for all of our users, at all levels, displayed on maps," said Geda. "As a powerful visualization tool, ArcGIS contributed to improved organization, justification of management decisions, and [the] warning and directing [of] residents through public awareness channels, which helped both government institutions and society."

FRD successfully deployed the local population warning and information system. Sirens alerted volunteers who participated in the drill about mandatory evacuations, while additional warning messages were sent to mobile phones and communicated on national television and radio broadcasts. Citizen volunteers within the exposed radius were efficiently evacuated, registered by authorities, washed, and given fresh clothing before being taken to safe locations for medical testing.

Additionally, the team was effective at launching the radiation hazard warning and monitoring information system (RADIS). Staff from FRD and its partner agencies harvested field data from municipalities via RIM apps, then analyzed and evaluated the results against their emergency exercise goals. Officials also held regular public briefings to provide citizens with the real-time status of simulation activities via an interactive map published to a public emergency website.

"All involved authorities across 19 different operational centers benefited from using the same operational tools from ArcGIS. This simplified all of our processes, including the gathering and arranging of real-time data displayed on shared operational maps and

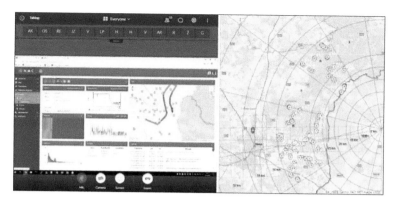

Participating agencies used maps and dashboards to display real-time information that helped with decision-making.

dashboards," said Geda. "Up-to-date information helped the FRD make well-informed decisions and in-time recommendations to exercise efficient public warnings."

Lithuania proves that it's ready

International observers from Latvia, Poland, Estonia, and the United Kingdom attended Lithuania's emergency nuclear simulation. Observers expressed an appreciation for the overall process, the arranged tools, and the technical capacities used to perform the simulation. Officials from the Ministry of the Interior and other national authorities in Lithuania recognized the FRD for successfully executing the emergency drill.

"The results of the exercises were very satisfying," said Geda. "All participating institutions gained valuable experience and stronger knowledge of the practical use of ArcGIS during the drills. We saw no issues concerning the processes, workflows, or the integrity of the data, thanks to the assistance provided by Hnit-Baltic representatives."

During the drill, citizens in the exposed radiation radius were evacuated, registered by authorities, washed, and given fresh clothes before receiving medical tests.

Lessons learned from the simulation have enabled the Lithuanian government to maximize its emergency preparedness and response efforts. Should a real nuclear incident occur, the FRD and partner agencies have the GIS tools and technology they need to support their plans to efficiently alert, inform, and evacuate Lithuanians to safety zones.

This story by Dave Fisse originally appeared as "In Lithuanian nuclear accident simulation, GIS delivers success" in the Spring 2020 issue of ArcNews. All images courtesy of Lithuanian Fire and Rescue Department unless otherwise noted.

FIRE DISTRICT USES APPS TO PREPARE FOR EMERGENCIES

Northwest Fire District, Tucson, Arizona

I N THE ARID DESERT LANDSCAPE OF SOUTHERN ARIZONA, where urban communities border wildlands, emergency preparedness is taking on a new urgency. The 2019–2020 fires in Australia and the many homes lost in California wildfire seasons remind firefighters and homeowners about the potential for catastrophic damage.

Firefighters at the Northwest Fire District (NWFD) in Tucson, Arizona, work to prevent fires and keep their community and its firefighters safe by inspecting hydrants and performing pre-incident planning. In addition, the NWFD team runs outreach programs and business inspections to help avoid injuries when fires do break out. To save lives and property when fire strikes, NWFD ensures firefighters can locate the closest hydrant, be certain it works, and determine

Quick action by the Northwest Fire District put out a brush fire that threatened nearby structures near La Cholla Boulevard and River Road on July 3, 2019.

whether hazardous materials are stored in the involved structure or any nearby buildings.

The NWFD team created mobile field apps, using a GIS, to speed up its inspection process and data collection—achieving a new level of hydrant inspection efficiency.

NWFD has delivered a direct monetary benefit for the community from its improved preparedness. Insurance companies review many safety-related parameters when setting rates, including measurements of functional water supply, such as hydrants. NWFD was given the highest classification possible in its most recent insurance evaluation, driving down the fire insurance rates—saving money for everyone in the district.

"The evolution from a paper-based system to field apps has been very well received," said Jim Long, senior GIS analyst at NWFD. "Going digital means firefighters can easily collect, upload, and view field data on their mobile devices."

Firefighters inspect every hydrant in the region every year and record the operational status on a mobile app.

Creating confidence in hydrants

NWFD's 11 fire stations serve a growing community of more than 110,000 people within a territory that spans more than 150 square miles. With very little surface water available, firefighters rely heavily on the operational status of every hydrant. They need to know the hydrant they will be using on scene is fully functional.

Now that NWFD has deployed mobile apps, every user can see the operational status of nearly 10,000 hydrants in real time.

"Our force can quickly and easily pinpoint the exact location of hydrants, verify they are fully functional, and identify the water companies responsible for each hydrant if they aren't working," Long said.

Firefighters inspect every hydrant in their region every year and record the operational status. In the past, they used paper forms and maps that resulted in more than 800 pages of handwritten notes held in large binders that firefighters carried around in their trucks during inspection season. Critical information on each hydrant was hard to update and was often inaccurate and inconsistent from truck to truck.

Using apps, the NWFD team was able to inspect and upload the real-time status of 4,000 hydrants in just 60 days—a workflow that makes hydrants more reliable and inspections transparent. "Seeing which hydrants are in what stage of inspection or repair on smart maps is huge because it allows us to track the progress in real time," said Tom Krinke, firefighter and paramedic with NWFD.

Making infrastructure inspections digital

Success with the hydrant app spurred the team to create and try purpose-built applications for additional preparedness tasks. A recent pilot test focused on pre-incident planning and risk assessment workflows, testing a mobile field app called the Pre-incident Plan Locator developed with Esri's assistance.

During the test, firefighters used the app to tailor surveys built to record the multi-hazard and integrated risk assessment workflows that are currently manual and paper based. The app recorded details about buildings, beyond the basic floor plans that get updated on an annual basis to produce hard copy maps.

As firefighters walk through a building inspection, they can pinpoint and mark physical assets in the app, such as the location of electric, gas, and water shutoffs; stairwells; elevators; or the alarm control panel. They can also assign a risk assessment score to each address. Structures are then color-coded on smart maps, providing an instant visual capture of the risk level, which firefighters can quickly reference in route to a fire.

With the app, if the structure is coded for higher risk, firefighters would be able to drill into more detailed data about the exact location of hazards before running into a building. The app was being evaluated for its potential to allow for such outcomes as safer navigation through a structure when smoke is heavy and visibility is low.

The prototype app could aid with practical decisions, such as where to park the fire truck, as it illuminates an 800-foot radius around a fire that corresponds to the length of the hoses on every truck. The app also identifies viable hydrants for the incident.

In the dry region of the US Southwest, NWFD firefighters will continue to battle blazes, protecting people and property using every advantage they can muster—including technology. The team's creative use of apps and smart maps have the potential to further improve preparedness.

"It's a matter of time before we take this pre-incident plan system to the next level, because fire captains only have 60 seconds to get all the information they need before each response," Long said.

Creating an app for everything

The passion to create and deploy mobile apps has gained momentum throughout NWFD for tasks once tackled by other systems and workflows.

Once the NWFD team realized the wealth of benefits apps provide firefighters in the field, it infused the technology into the firehouses. This has improved daily life and work inside and outside the firehouses.

"We've created a new conceptual map-based Facilities Repair Request system that we're piloting in one station to track the repair status of all assets, such as refrigerators, dishwashers, coffee pots, and the other stuff inside our facilities," said Long. "If something breaks, the app lets our firefighters record the problem, which creates a task for our maintenance personnel to fix it."

The interactive floor plan in the Pre-incident Plan Locator app prototype has the potential to enhance firefighter awareness and safety when smoke blocks their vision.

The system is built using a suite of mobile software from Esri that includes ArcGIS Survey123 with its simple form-centric data gathering tools, ArcGIS Collector for field data collection, and ArcGIS Workforce that coordinates work management assignments.

Having all the information about each asset in the system, such as manufacturer and serial numbers, saves time for the maintenance team. The app also provides a central system to track the types of repairs across the district and the maintenance cost per facility or shift.

The eagerness to create more purpose-built apps extends beyond work for some users.

"Just for fun, I've used it for home renovation work and, currently, we use it for our grocery shopping," said Krinke. "I created an app with my personal account that allows my kids to simply touch a button when we run out of something, and it creates an open task for me. Anytime I'm near the grocery store, it alerts me and tells me what I need to get."

This story by Mike Cox originally appeared as "Northwest Fire District Embraces Apps to Better Prepare for Emergencies" on the Esri Blog on February 20, 2020. All images courtesy of Northwest Fire District, Tucson, Arizona, unless otherwise noted.

GETTING STARTED WITH GIS

GIS MAPPING AND ANALYTICS ESTABLISHES A COLLABORA-tion pattern across emergency management organizations. Below are some recommended steps to help you be better prepared. You can find links to the resources mentioned in this section on the book web page at **go.esri.com/dwd-resources.**

Identify preparedness data

Gather and map your foundational data in your area. These layers include basic infrastructure and administrative areas:

- Structures and structure type (single-family homes, multi-family units, commercial, etc.)
- Major facilities and landmarks (schools, malls, places of worship, parks, stadiums, etc.)
- Health infrastructure (hospitals, clinics, assisted living facilities, etc.)
- Public safety infrastructure (police stations, fire stations, etc.)
- Shelters
- Roads
- Bridges
- Dams
- Utilities
- Communications infrastructure
- Water features (lakes, streams, rivers, etc.)
- Parcels
- Addresses

- Administrative boundaries
- Population and demographics

Include hazard-specific data that is relevant for your area of interest. If you are unsure of what hazards present the greatest risk in your area, tools such as FEMA's Resilience Analysis and Planning Tool (RAPT) in the United States can help you assess priorities:

- Wildfires
- Floods
- Earthquakes
- Hurricanes
- Storm surge
- Severe weather
- Crime
- Health

Add ready-to-use, curated content from ArcGIS Living Atlas of the World. It contains many ready-to-use "live feeds" that provide dynamic, real-time information that can be used in addition to the local data previously mentioned:

- Weather feeds
- Disaster feeds
- Earth observation feeds
- Multispectral feeds

Also consider adding real-time services for additional situational awareness:

- National Shelter System
- World Traffic Service
- WAZE traffic

Identify data gaps

Once you have the base data above collected and organized, it's time to assess where you are—to identify data gaps. The data drill is a multi-organization exercise used to gain insight into how a community collectively thinks about, manages, shares, and uses data during an emergency.

Data drills are developed and conducted based on operational challenges involving data and are a valuable tool for disaster preparedness. Data drills can be designed around a specific scenario relevant to your community such as flooding, fire, or earthquake to ensure you are planning for all data needs.

Here are a few things to consider in your data drill. Once you've considered these things, develop a plan to collect or create data where required based on these tasks:

- ☐ Detail your organization-specific operational workflows and use cases based on the scenario.

- ☐ Identify the relevant decisions that are needed and what datasets, including metadata and data dictionaries, support those key decisions.

- ☐ Look next at your interagency workflows based on the scenario and do the same—identify the key decisions and support data needs.

☐ For each data point, identify the responsible organization contacts, roles, and responsibilities for this dataset.

☐ Identify whether any data sharing agreements will be needed between partners and start collecting and sharing the data identified in this drill.

Create and share maps

After locating the needed data sources, you can create a variety of maps to help prepare your community for emergencies. Consider these tasks in your mapmaking:

☐ **Map capacity:** Map your facilities, infrastructure, employees or citizens, medical resources, equipment, goods, and services to understand and prepare to respond to potential emergencies.

☐ **Map hazards:** Create maps showing the location of hazards that could potentially impact your community, such as seismic vulnerability, flood zones, and wildfire potential.

☐ **Map vulnerable populations:** Map social vulnerability, age, and other factors to monitor at-risk groups in the regions you serve during an emergency.

☐ **Share maps:** Share your maps with your community on your website. Increasing community understanding of potential hazards can help prevent serious damage and deaths if and when disaster strikes.

Share preparedness plans with your community

Sharing your emergency preparedness plans with the community helps citizens understand risks, increases readiness, provides transparency, and improves adoption and success rates. Here are some examples of organizations communicating their mitigation strategies to increase emergency preparedness in their communities:

- **Ottawa, Ohio: A mitigation success story:** Major flooding is a frequent occurrence in Ottawa, Ohio. Officials acquired and demolished repeatedly flooded properties as a mitigation tool.

- **MDOT metro region flood mitigation projects:** In 2017, the Michigan Department of Transportation (MDOT) allocated $5.4 million to help mitigate flooding in the Detroit Metro Region.

- **Ohio Safe Room Rebate Program:** The Ohio Safe Room Rebate Program provides a rebate for the purchase and construction or installation of tornado safe rooms for homeowners.

- **Are You Ready, Tampa Bay?:** The City of Tampa's Local Mitigation Strategy identifies 20 hazards that pose a risk to the city.

Follow best practices

Ensure that your maps and apps are ready to handle the load from the public and news media, and that your GIS environment is ready for the next response.

Essential configurations for highly scalable (viral) ArcGIS Online web applications

ArcGIS Online is built on reliable, scalable infrastructure that supports the massive amount of web traffic that viral applications receive.

Learn by doing

Hands-on learning will strengthen your understanding of GIS and how it can be used to improve disaster preparedness. Learn ArcGIS, a collection of free story-driven lessons such as the ones listed here, allows you to experience GIS when it is applied to real-life problems:

- **Introduction to ArcGIS Online:** Get started with web mapping with ArcGIS Online.

- **Integrate maps, apps, and scenes to tell a story:** Share information about earthquake risk using maps, apps, and scenes.

- **Identify landslide risk areas in Colorado:** Analyze a map to predict mudflows in rain-soaked Colorado.

- **Protect your home from wildfires by calculating defensible space:** Calculate the home ignition zone for a building in the fire-prone San Bernardino National Forest.

Get there faster with GIS templates

Esri's disaster preparedness templates, such as the ones listed here, help you quickly assemble critical data, create relevant maps, and share important information:

- **Organize foundational data:** You can use this collection of GIS maps and apps to aggregate and share data used throughout the emergency management life cycle.

- **Initiate flood planning:** Emergency management personnel use this map to analyze the impact of seasonal flooding scenarios and develop flood response plans.

- **Become more resilient:** Emergency management agencies can use this collection of maps and apps to prepare for the impact of acute shocks and chronic stresses on the community.

- **Engage the public:** The public uses these GIS maps and apps to understand hazards in the community and locate assistance if an incident occurs.

Learn more

For additional resources and links to live examples, visit the book web page at **go.esri.com/dwd-resources**.

PART 2

DISASTER RESPONSE

EMERGENCY MANAGEMENT PROFESSIONALS DEPEND ON timely and accurate information to manage disasters and large-scale emergencies with foresight and agility. When disasters occur, GIS empowers the critical decision-making that can help you save lives and property. Real-time tools help you maintain situational and operational awareness, analyze incident impact, assess damage, deploy resources, and inform the public.

Stay ahead of changing conditions

Maintain real-time situational awareness in an emergency. Monitor changing conditions and brief your teams using the latest information.

Assess damage

Understand the potential impact to your community and accurately assess damage in the field so you can deploy resources where they are needed and access recovery funds as quickly as possible.

Share critical, up-to-date public information

Report current conditions and response actions to the public, media, and affected organizations using maps, dashboards, and story maps that provide location-based context that drives action.

GIS in action

In this section, we'll look at real-life stories of how organizations use GIS to respond to emergencies; we'll also provide you with recommended steps for implementing GIS in your organization.

TRACKING CORONAVIRUS WITH REAL-TIME DASHBOARDS

Johns Hopkins University's Center for Systems Science and Engineering

A S PANDEMIC FEARS ESCALATED IN LATE JANUARY 2020, Johns Hopkins University published its now-famous coronavirus disease 2019 (COVID-19) dashboard—a map-based tool developed to track and fight the spread of COVID-19. Developed by Lauren Gardner and her team from the University's Center for Systems Science and Engineering, the dashboard went viral almost instantly, with many news articles and shares on social media and hundreds of millions of page views.

While it's clear the dashboard—with real-time information about the global health emergency—is immensely popular, it takes some analysis to understand why.

The health-care community has used maps to understand the spread of disease for a long time, most famously in 1854 when Dr. John Snow connected location and illness with his history-making map of a London cholera outbreak. From disease atlases of the early 20th century to more recent web-mapping of Ebola and Zika outbreaks, health-care professionals have long considered mapping, and more recently, geographic information systems (GIS), critical tools in tracking and combating contagion.

The movement of disease and data

One of the greatest challenges in the war against disease is humanity's increasing mobility. Today, a person can pick up a virus in one place and share it to any other location on the planet within hours. Among

The World Health Organization (WHO) has created a dashboard to track the global spread of COVID-19 cases. (Static screen shot as of March 20, 2020.)

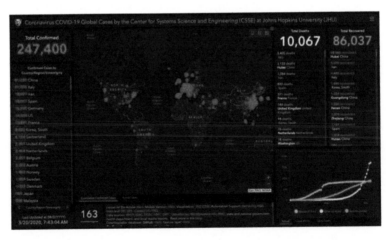

Johns Hopkins University is tracking the spread of COVID-19 cases in near real time with a map-centric dashboard using ArcGIS Online that pulls relevant data from WHO, US CDC, ECDC, China CDC (CCDC), NHC, and Dingxiangyuan. (Static screen shot as of March 20, 2020.)

airline travelers, there's the potential to become a super spreader, infecting a large number of people across a large geographic area.

This level of mobility places scientists at a serious disadvantage in slowing potential epidemics. While technology to create vaccines has become incredibly advanced, it still takes months to formulate an effective vaccine for a new virus. In those months, the virus can easily reach every corner of the world.

When disease can travel so quickly, information has to move even faster. The intense response generated by the Johns Hopkins dashboard shows how eager people are to track health threats around the world. The dashboard presents targeted, up-to-date information needed to understand the progress of a disease and makes it available in a public, easy-to-digest format. Anyone with access to the internet can learn, in a few short clicks, a tremendous amount about the novel coronavirus and COVID-19 disease.

The dashboard's interactive map includes the number of confirmed infections, fatalities, and recoveries, and where they happened. Graphs detail the progress of the virus over time. Viewers can also see the day and time of the most recent data update and review the data sources used to produce the dashboard.

Five authoritative sources selected by Johns Hopkins for the effort include the World Health Organization, the Centers for Disease Control and Prevention, the National Health Commission of the People's Republic of China, the European Centre for Disease Prevention and Control, and the online medical resource DXY.cn. The Johns Hopkins dashboard provides links to these authoritative sources where viewers can learn more.

Web services allow GIS users to easily ingest and display disparate data inputs without having to host or process the data centrally. This eases data sharing and speeds the aggregation of information for improved understanding.

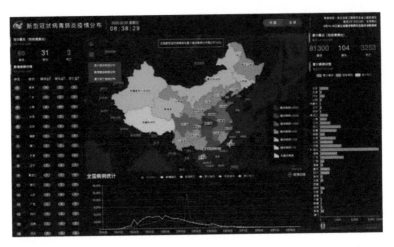

The Chinese Center for Disease Control and Prevention tracks the spread of COVID-19 cases across China. Updates come from the National Health Commission and its provincial health organizations. (Static screen shot as of March 20, 2020.)

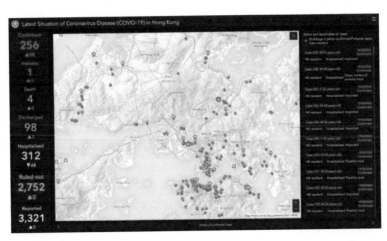

The Hong Kong dashboard shows the locations of buildings visited by higher concentrations of confirmed COVID-19 cases and the locations of current quarantines—a detail that can help residents of those areas actively reduce their exposure. (Static screen shot as of March 20, 2020.)

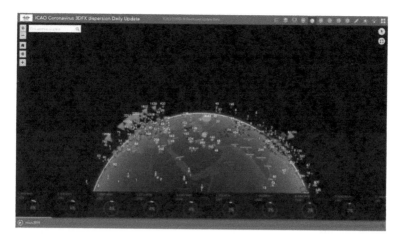

The International Civil Aviation Organization created an animated dashboard to convey typical air traffic connectivity in different parts of the world compared with current COVID-19 cases. This resource illustrates the potential for quick spread, given today's increased mobility. (Static screen shot as of March 20, 2020.)

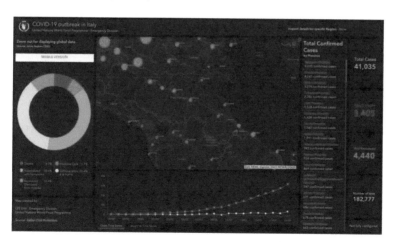

The United Nations World Food Programme created this dashboard of confirmed COVID-19 cases and the total population affected in Italy. (Static screen shot as of March 20, 2020.)

More dashboards share localized details

Since the release of the Johns Hopkins dashboard, other organizations have been quick to use GIS technology to address similar needs. The resulting dashboards share some of the same details, customized with additional information to serve specific audiences.

Several of these tools, like the one created by Johns Hopkins, include a mobile-optimized version, which makes the dashboards more versatile and accessible to the public on phones and tablets.

Technology's potential for disease control

In the future, one could imagine dashboards being used to direct citizens of affected areas to the locations of crucial aid and resources. Dashboard maps could identify hospitals with available beds, clinics offering medical aid along with the current wait times, grocery stores and pharmacies that are open, where to purchase personal protective equipment, and so on. In heavily impacted cities, this kind of information could critically improve outcomes and save lives.

Future disease dashboards could incorporate the locations of scheduled cultural events and celebrations to accurately reflect the associated risk to travelers and enhance public health decision-making. By bringing together location and time-sensitive events in relationship to a spreading disease, officials have the potential to reduce exposure and spread.

Disease shapes decisions

The arrival of COVID-19, like pandemics in the past, impacted the way people travel, the way people feed themselves, and the economy.

As human mobility spread the coronavirus at an unprecedented pace, outbreaks brought affected communities to a standstill, and anxiety stretched across the globe.

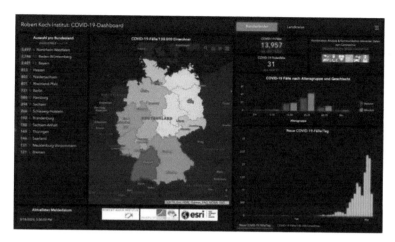

The Robert Koch Institute created this dashboard to show the number of COVID-19 cases in Germany. (Static screen shot as of March 20, 2020.)

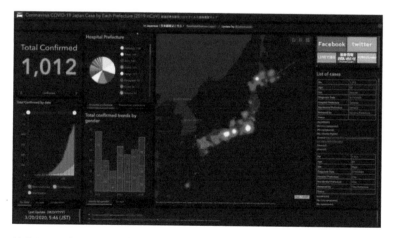

JAG Japan Corp created this dashboard to show the number of COVID-19 cases by prefecture in Japan. (Static screen shot as of March 20, 2020.)

The public health community remains hard at work finding new ways to combat the current threat while the medical community and governments rally to provide treatments, find cures, and distribute vaccines to the world population. The availability of real-time, map-based dashboards have a role to play in informing all of these actions. This method of communication provides accessible, easily under-stood information to people around the world eager to protect them-selves and their communities. This tool improves data transparency and helps authorities efficiently and effectively disseminate informa-tion to improve awareness about quickly spreading diseases.

A version of this story by Este Geraghty, MD, MS, MPH, GISP, originally appeared as "Coronavirus: World Connectivity Can Save Lives" on the Esri Blog on February 18, 2020.

APPS TRANSFORM HURRICANE RESPONSE

Geographic Mapping Technologies, Corp.

AFTER HURRICANE MARIA ROARED THROUGH PUERTO RICO on September 20, 2017, the island was in a state of total chaos. The category 4 storm destroyed the power grid, leaving all 3.4 million residents without electricity. The storm decimated already-aged infrastructure, rendering many roads and bridges unusable; and it devastated communication networks, cutting off internet and cell service almost completely.

Disaster response and recovery efforts were going to be difficult. The unincorporated US territory, which declared bankruptcy that May, hadn't even recuperated from Hurricane Irma, a category 5 storm that grazed the island two weeks prior and left 80,000 people without power.

Once everyone in Puerto Rico was able to get out of their houses and make sure their families were safe—which took a few days—the central government set up an Emergency Operations Center (COE in Spanish) at the convention center in the capital city of San Juan. From there, a number of different organizations began coordinating efforts to restore the power grid, fix roads and bridges, get medical aid and disaster relief to residents, and assess the damage. But with all forms of digital and mobile communication down, they were going to need to get creative.

When staff from Geographic Mapping Technologies, Corp. (GMT), got to the COE, they saw that the organizations were working pretty independently of one another. Many agencies had brought GIS teams, so they were making their own maps and printing a lot of them out to take into the field. Additionally, everyone seemed to have separate maps of key locations: cell towers, gas stations, hospitals, and supermarkets. That wasn't going to get anything done quickly. So GMT, Esri's official distributor in Puerto Rico, stepped in.

Even though all the agencies and organizations at the Emergency Operations Center (COE) coordinated their efforts with GIS, disaster recovery still moved slowly in Puerto Rico. Photo courtesy of Aurelio Castro.

With assistance from Esri's Disaster Response Program (DRP), staff from GMT not only integrated everyone's GIS resources into one place, but they also built innovative apps that field crews could use to collect and share data—even offline. This made the response go much faster than it would have otherwise.

"And that's so strange because, for us (the residents of Puerto Rico), it took forever," said Glenda Román, GMT's professional services manager.

Data all over the place

No one in Puerto Rico anticipated that the aftermath of Hurricane Maria would be as bad as it was.

"We didn't expect to be with everything one day and then nothing the next day," said Diego Llamas, the technical support manager for GMT. "Communications, the internet, and all the facilities you have using your cell phone—those didn't work."

This was a huge problem for the organizations orchestrating the response.

With help from Esri's Disaster Response Program (DRP), staff from GMT got about 90 percent of the organizations at the COE doing their GIS work in ArcGIS. Photo courtesy of Aurelio Castro.

"Their own apps worked in the field only if there was internet or [a] mobile connection," said Alberto Millán, a GIS analyst for GMT. "When they got to Puerto Rico, they had problems because there was no service."

Scrambling to get their operations under way, the various GIS units started printing out maps—hundreds, maybe thousands of them. The GMT team noticed immediately that this was causing many agencies to duplicate efforts.

"Data was all over the place, and nobody was getting that data," recalled Román.

GMT's president, Aurelio (Tito) Castro, agreed with the planning board that everyone needed to start collaborating—quickly—and begin using the same dynamic data to get a robust response going.

The Puerto Rico Planning Board already had an ArcGIS Online account, so Castro interfaced with the DRP team—which reached out to him the day after the hurricane to offer GMT any help it needed—to get extra licenses and credits.

"The first thing we did was set up as a hub through the ArcGIS Online account for the Puerto Rico Planning Board," said Román.

"Since that day, we started growing the users in the planning board's system, [and everyone] started putting information into the common platform," added Castro.

"We connected all these agencies through creating groups and sharing content," continued Román. "By doing that, we were able to provide one space where all these first responders could gather local data [on] roads, hospitals, gas stations, supermarkets, [and] criminal incidents."

They also started receiving a steady stream of documents and links from the DRP that contained data, images, and apps from people around the Esri community who were working to help Puerto Rico with the response.

"The [DRP] was very, very helpful in providing us with other data that we were not aware had been published by other groups, including services, aerial photographs, [and] information published by federal agencies," said Castro.

To continue getting the GIS support it needed, GMT was in constant communication with the DRP in the days and weeks following the hurricane.

"We had many conversations via text in the middle of the night just to get things up and running," said Brenda Martinez, the disaster response and public safety marketing specialist at Esri.

"It's very important that people around the world understand that Esri has this capability 24/7," said Castro, adding that he called for support at all hours, even on weekends.

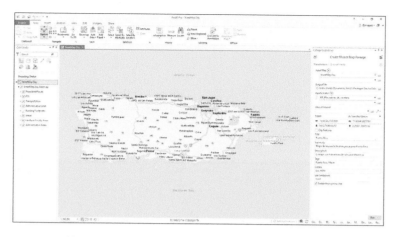

Because addressing in Puerto Rico's rural areas is tricky, Geographic Mapping Technologies, Corp. (GMT), built a composite locator based on data from various agencies and used building and landowner names to geocode locations.

A special locator and a customized app

After deploying ArcGIS Online as a hub, the next issue was getting these agencies and organizations off paper maps and onto mobile apps so they could coordinate more seamlessly.

"All these people needed to move in the field, and that's why they were requesting paper maps," recalled Román.

But even with paper maps, rescue and recovery workers were having a hard time finding the addresses they were looking for. That's because addressing outside city centers in Puerto Rico is complicated.

"In urban areas, it would work just as in the US, with street names and numbers," said Román. "But once you get...in the rural areas, you won't have house numbers or even street names."

Instead, the main thoroughfares are numbered state roads that have markers at each kilometer. From there, interior roads branch out like limbs on a tree.

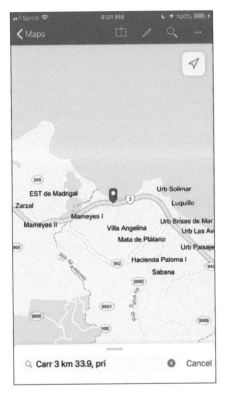

Using a customized version of ArcGIS Explorer, first responders were able to find what they were looking for in rural areas based on the kilometer markers on state roads.

"The closest you can get to a physical address is the kilometer. From that point onward, you have to use references and ask people how to get around," explained Román. "That's the biggest challenge that first responders faced—because how do you reach those areas if you don't have an address?"

The lack of internet and mobile connectivity made this worse. But GMT staff had a solution in mind; it would just take a bit of rigging.

Esri had already worked with GMT to improve geocoding so it was more compatible with the needs in Puerto Rico's rural areas.

"We built a special locator for them where they could type in the distance—0.1 kilometers, 0.2 kilometers—along the road and find that location," said Jeff Rogers, the geocoding program manager at Esri. "We'd built this capability for them into online services, and they've been using that for years. But when the internet went down, we needed to pull together a local, offline solution."

Several teams at Esri worked with GMT for about a week to build a custom search capability, along with a customized version of the ArcGIS Explorer app, that would enable first responders to go out into rural areas with handheld devices to find and report on people who needed assistance and incidents that required attention—all without internet or cell connectivity. This entailed building a composite locator based on all sorts of data from different agencies and using parcel data to build the geocoder by name.

"We didn't have addresses, but we did have the names of who owns the land. So we geocoded the names," explained Román. "Then, once you get to the kilometer, you can actually figure out how to move to [a] house by identifying the owner's name."

This proved indispensable to getting field crews out to their assignments so they could provide support and do inspections of damaged infrastructure and buildings.

"This was a good test for the disconnected functionality because there was actually no internet, and it worked superbly," added Román.

Different agencies, different needs

GMT's work didn't stop there. The team built six custom apps in total and collaborated with all the organizations at the COE to get them the GIS services and apps they needed.

"With different agencies, we had different jobs," recalled Llamas. "One of them asked for the geocoding. Other ones asked for surveys. Other ones wanted to collect information."

In addition to Explorer, the team employed ArcGIS Survey123, ArcGIS Collector, ArcGIS Web AppBuilder, and ArcGIS Dashboards to help each agency and organization get its work done more efficiently.

The US Army Corps of Engineers, for example, inspected a lot of infrastructure and provided direct aid to residents. Its team members employed the customized Explorer app to figure out where to land helicopters in rural areas and determine how bad the damage was to houses and other structures.

The CDC benefited from having the four or five paper-based forms it was using entered into ArcGIS Survey123 so it could gather and disseminate health data digitally rather than running paperwork back and forth across the island.

The GMT team also helped municipalities digitize their data collection efforts and workflows. Staff at the Caguas municipality, for example, wanted to track their progress with clearing roads of downed trees and garbage. They also wanted to update citizens on which roads and bridges were open for transit and which ones weren't.

"We made dashboards and web maps for them, and they used ArcGIS Pro," said Millán.

Once the team from GMT got going, most of the apps took just 10–45 minutes to build, while the more complicated ones required, at most, two or three days. Soon, about 90 percent of the organizations at the COE were using ArcGIS technology, according to Castro's estimate.

"We had to do more with fewer resources, and ArcGIS was crucial to that," he reflected.

Residents of Puerto Rico have no historic memory of facing a hurricane as bad as Maria. Photo courtesy of Aurelio Castro.

A platform that made the difference

With all the agencies using GIS apps both in the field and back at the COE, local police sharing crime data almost constantly, the transportation agency updating people on road conditions every day, and everyone receiving additional data through the DRP—all in ArcGIS, and all without connectivity in the field—disaster response efforts picked up. But things still moved slowly.

"Typically, the response phase lasts a couple of days to a couple of weeks," said Jeff Baranyi, Esri's public safety assistance program operations manager. "For Puerto Rico, they were in response mode for several months. The whole [territory] seemed to be relatively crippled. The magnitude of damage was quite vast."

It took the Puerto Rico Electric Power Authority 11 months to report complete power restoration. Washed out roads and bridges needed to be repaired. And a study from George Washington University's Milken Institute School of Public Health estimated that in the six months after Hurricane Maria struck, anywhere from 2,658 to 3,290 excess deaths occurred due to the extended relief and recovery process.

"The hurricane was way beyond any historic memory there is here in Puerto Rico," said Román. "But using ArcGIS was a way of bringing together all the agencies, of sharing data on Puerto Rico, [and] of helping organize the response efforts and then the recovery efforts. Everything could be easily deployed, and so fast—no programming needed. And I think that really made a difference. Without that, the response would have been slower than what it actually was."

A version of this story by Citabria Stevens originally appeared in the Fall 2018 issue of ArcNews. All images courtesy of Geographic Mapping Technologies, Corp., unless otherwise noted.

GIS SUPPORTS RESPONSE TO HURRICANE IRMA

City of Fort Lauderdale, Florida

WHEN HURRICANE IRMA FIRST MADE LANDFALL IN THE Florida Keys on September 10, 2017, it brought destructive 70 mph winds and storm surges and left widespread power outages and downed trees and debris on Florida streets.

The city of Fort Lauderdale, located on the east coast of Florida, is no stranger to major weather events, and the city's GIS provided vital information to public safety, public works, and other departments so city staff could quickly but safely respond to residents' needs during the event and support recovery efforts after the storm had passed.

"The city showed that it was well prepared for an event like Irma, and GIS was crucial to that preparedness," said Ian Wint, GIS manager for Fort Lauderdale. "The EOC (Emergency Operations Center) and its occupants have become increasingly reliant on GIS and the way it presents information. EOC occupants often leaned on GIS as the first source for information. It's telling that for about the first three or four hours of the recovery, EOC occupants requested that all seven large displays in the EOC show a GIS application. Perhaps just as impressive was the reality that GIS staff printed no more than five or six maps in the five days the EOC was activated. Staff were more interested in interactive solutions."

The GIS Division used ArcGIS Online, ArcGIS Online application templates, ArcGIS StoryMaps apps, and the regular edition of ArcGIS Web AppBuilder to compile and analyze data and disseminate information on the status of the hurricane, city infrastructure, and response efforts. Customized web apps embedded in a StoryMaps

Flooding in the city of Fort Lauderdale after Hurricane Irma in September 2017.

app called the Emergency Operations Portal gave staff from various city departments and work units access to information relevant to their responsibilities. A simple symbolization scheme allowed them to monitor the status of hurricane-related issues: open issues were red, in-progress issues were yellow, and closed issues were green.

In addition to its own GIS data and existing apps, Fort Lauderdale had access to relatively current high-resolution aerials as well as shelter and evacuation zone information from Broward County.

Prior to Irma making landfall and especially after the storm passed, the GIS Division relied on LauderServ (also known as QAlert), its 311-like system, to crowdsource information. City residents and staff use the system to report nonemergency issues via its web page, mobile app, or by telephone. Requests from LauderServ are pulled into ArcGIS in real time and served out in a web app. City work units can filter requests to identify ones that fall in their area of responsibility.

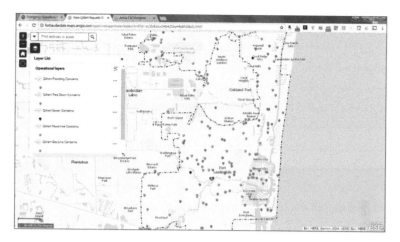

Fort Lauderdale relied on LauderServ (also known as QAlert), its 311-like system, to crowdsource information.

Decision makers in the EOC were granted real-time access to LauderServ requests via an ArcGIS Online viewer app. Fire-rescue, police, public works, and other department staff needed request information to provide aid to residents as quickly as possible and effectively coordinate field activities.

During the second day of the Irma response, a member of the fire-rescue command staff observed that an interactive mapping interface would allow for querying and filtering data and provide a better view of 911 calls than the interface and access method available to them at the time. As a result, a web app was developed using Web AppBuilder that map enabled the 911 dispatch system. Using internal 911 calls for service data, the location and priority calls for service were mapped, color-coded, and annotated with a priority code.

"The application showing fire-rescue and police calls for service was born from years of working with the Fire-Rescue Department and showing them what is possible," said Wint. "By map enabling the 911 dispatch system in this way, command staff gained greater insight into storm-related incidents, such as two cases of breaking and entering of commercial properties that occurred before the storm's arrival."

During the early stages of Irma, data on wind speed was critical to ensuring the safety of city staff involved in response efforts. The city used map services that provided Esri live feeds of National Oceanic and Atmospheric Administration (NOAA) data on wind speed and direction and NOAA storm reports. When conditions permitted staff to respond, sustained wind speeds and recorded gust data helped determine the most appropriate type of vehicle to use.

GIS also made sensor data from the utility operations supervisory control and data acquisition (SCADA) system actionable and helped utility staff manage the pumps and pressure of the city's wastewater system during the storm. Heavy rain and floodwater from a major storm can drain through surface level manholes and into the wastewater system. If this happens in areas where pump stations are malfunctioning, it can result in sewage backups that reach the surface.

Inside the Emergency Operations Center (EOC).

Utility staff members used a web-based editor application created by the GIS Division to enter SCADA information in the GIS. As the storm progressed, EOC occupants and utility managers monitored the status and capacity of the sewer pump stations through the use of a viewer app. They watched as the interactive map, initially mostly green, became dominated with red. With constantly updated information on which pump stations were experiencing power failure and approaching capacity limits, decision makers could quickly respond to this situation after the storm.

A powerful storm such as Irma leaves hazards that must be dealt with promptly. If Broward County activates its EOC as the result of a severe weather event, each municipality must conduct a Rapid Impact Assessment (RIA) once it is safe to do so. To systematically perform the RIA, Broward County is divided into grids, each one a quarter mile in size.

Municipalities performed the RIA as a quick drive-by inspection, or survey, to assess any damage that has been sustained and provide a numerical rating for the wind and flood damage sustained in each grid in their jurisdiction. The rating scale ranges from 0 (no damage) to 4 (catastrophic damage). The field information gathered by the RIA helped managers better understand needs so they can make better-informed decisions when deploying resources.

In Fort Lauderdale, the Fire-Rescue and building inspection staffs joined to conduct this assessment. The Fort Lauderdale RIA Viewer, a web mapping app, was used by the EOC to track damage incidents throughout the city as they were reported.

The GIS Division has an ongoing role supporting the city's disaster preparedness plan. Each year, Fort Lauderdale conducts at least one mock exercise. The GIS Division uses that event as an opportunity to learn more about the EOC's needs and educate staff about GIS capabilities.

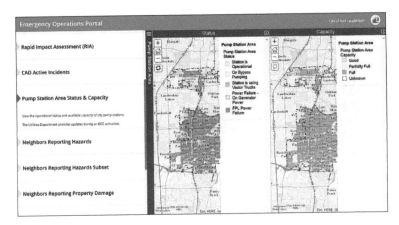

EOC occupants and utility managers were kept abreast of the status and capacity of sewer pump stations through the use of this viewer app available from the Emergency Operations Portal.

With every disaster, the GIS Division learns more. During Hurricane Matthew in 2016, the GIS Division created apps based on ArcGIS templates during the event. Following Hurricane Irma, there have been requests to retain the Fire-Rescue and Police Calls for Service app that was created during Hurricane Irma. Although the SCADA network is currently separated from the city's regular network, post-Irma there is a strong interest in modifying the network design to allow GIS to read directly from SCADA without human intervention in a way that does not make the utility networks vulnerable to security exploits.

The GIS Division effectively helped the city deal with Hurricane Irma, in part, because it has been developing a solid portfolio of solutions over many years that have improved the city's processes while building relationships with city departments. When Wint joined the city in 1999, he doubled the city's GIS staff. The GIS coordinator since 2000, Wint has overseen the steady growth of GIS at Fort Lauderdale.

Post-storm activity starts at dawn with the Rapid Impact Assessment of the entire city. Decision makers in the EOC received real-time access to the status of the assessments via this viewer application.

That growth has been enhanced in recent years by a strategy of embracing Web GIS. Wint explained the reasons behind this strategy. "The GIS Division has always viewed web technology as a way to serve more customers and in a way that is usually more efficient than solely relying on desktop technology or as an order desk. The default mindset when developing a solution to a problem or displaying results is to first ask the question of whether it would be appropriate for a web application. The web offers many advantages, including allowing us to reach a wider audience."

Not only can the GIS Division reach more users using web technology, but it can also reach them at a lower cost to the city because web-based solutions are centrally maintained.

To multiply the impact of each solution, the GIS Division introduces new apps or enhanced services in a way that encourages city staff to see new uses for the technology. The division sends the announcement via email to every city staff member.

"So, staff in engineering may see the announcement for a new application we created for transportation and mobility even though

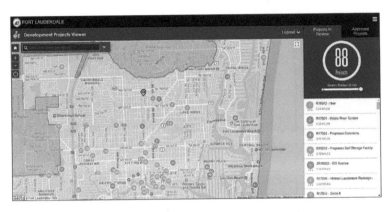

Because Fort Lauderdale GIS notifies all city departments of new apps it develops, city staff often find that apps built for one purpose can be used for another. LauderStreet, which provides information on scheduled road closures, was reworked to become LauderWorks, for tracking city-managed construction and repair projects, and then became the Development Project Viewer, which shows land development projects in the city's review system.

on the surface the new application may not concern engineering," Wint said. "This does two things: first, it reminds engineering and others that GIS exists within the city; and second, it gives them ideas on a solution created for one work group [that] can benefit their work group."

Wint saw that happen when the LauderStreet app was released. LauderStreet provides location and other information on scheduled road closures. It morphed into LauderWorks, which lets residents know about city-managed construction and repair projects. LauderStreet had yet another reincarnation when the Urban Design and Planning Department requested the GIS staff spin off an app called Development Project Viewer that shows land development projects in the city's review system.

These and other projects that the GIS Division undertakes support its overarching goal of making local government more efficient.

It strives to empower the city with tools to access the most accurate, timely, and useful information—especially information that might not otherwise be easily accessed—through user-friendly graphic interfaces.

These tools become even more valuable to the city when responding to events such as Hurricane Irma.

A version of this story by Monica Pratt originally appeared as "Fort Lauderdale's GIS Supports Response to Hurricane Irma" in the Fall 2017 issue of *ArcNews*. All images courtesy of City of Fort Lauderdale, Florida, unless otherwise noted.

SCIENTISTS, EMERGENCY RESPONDERS PUT DRONES TO WORK

Center for Robot-Assisted Search and Rescue

WITH FIERY LAVA FLOW FROM HAWAI'I'S ERUPTING Kīlauea volcano prompting urgent evacuation orders in 2018, one might expect the last thing on residents' minds would be cleaning house (the volcano erupted again in December 2020). Yet, many locals of Leilani Estates, a neighborhood now mostly destroyed, not only took the time to clean their homes, they also did extra gardening, planted fresh flowers, and left offerings to honor the volcano that was threatening their homes.

The Hawaiian people pay homage to Pele, the volcano goddess, by leaving offerings to be burned up as the lava advances.

This last-minute preparation paid respect to Pele, the Hawaiian volcano goddess. Kīlauea continues to wreak havoc in spectacular fashion, spewing billions of gallons of molten lava across the landscape of Hawai'i's Big Island and into the ocean. But the Hawaiian people are pragmatic and accepting, viewing Pele's activity as part of the natural process of destruction and creation that forms the Hawaiian Islands. They clean their homes to return them to Pele in a good state, since they believe she gave them the land in the first place.

This ongoing eruption of the Kīlauea volcano, which started in early May 2018, continues to shock geologists. The US Geological Survey (USGS) notes that such an event is unprecedented in the past 200 years. The Halema'uma'u crater has grown to seven times its previous size by volume, creating almost 700 acres of new land. Hundreds of homes were destroyed. In the first days of the eruption, evacuations and search and rescue operations included a drone strike team.

First (robot) responders

Among those responding to the volcanic eruption were a new breed of emergency responders: robots from the Center for Robot-Assisted Search and Rescue, or CRASAR. A five-person team of highly trained volunteers from CRASAR deployed to Kīlauea a few days after the eruption. They brought a fleet of small remotely piloted aircraft, commonly known as drones, to assist in the rescue operations.

CRASAR, a nonprofit organization, champions the use of small drones in emergency response. Disasters present dangerous and sometimes life-threatening scenarios to first responders. Disaster robots can go where people or emergency response dogs can't, minimizing the risk to life. CRASAR assisted at the World Trade Center after the 9/11 attack and since then has supplied robotic assistance for 28 disasters, including earthquakes, building collapses, floods, nuclear accidents, tsunamis, and underground mine explosions.

Kīlauea provided a new challenge to the team, and they executed the first known use of drones in emergency response to a volcanic eruption. While drones had been used previously to map volcanoes, CRASAR's fleet was the first to use them to officially aid disaster response. The team's participation also freed up drone resources from the University of Hawaiʻi at Hilo to focus on geological observations during those crucial first days.

Breaking this new ground made an impact on the experienced team. Justin Adams, president of CRASAR, described their encounter with Pele vividly:

"It was unique. I've never dealt with lava before. None of us have. We've dealt with mudslides, and we tried to compare it to mudslides. But just the color of the lava, the sparkling of it burning up the vegetation and trees, looked like blood flowing down the side of the mountain. It looked like arteries because of the way it was pulsing."

Ground truth by drone

During a six-day period, from May 14 to May 19, 2018, CRASAR flew 44 drone flights, 16 of which happened at night. These missions were invaluable, since piloted aircraft such as helicopters were prohibited to fly at night. The crew staged the drone flights from restricted-access roads near the volcano, driving their vehicle through the eerily quiet evacuation zones and moving locations often to follow and map the lava flows.

During these flights, the drones were outfitted with thermal sensors. They identified a new fissure (Fissure 8, which continued to expel lava months later), mapped the lava fronts using thermal cameras, and provided data to the USGS to help determine the speed of lava flow.

To capture the data, a drone would hover above the front edge of a lava flow, take an image straight down, and note the GPS coordinate of that image. Several minutes later, the drone would follow the leading edge of the flow to its new location and repeat the procedure. This was a much safer maneuver than previous USGS data collection, according to Adams.

"They had been gathering data by a person getting close to the lava, taking a GPS coordinate, waiting, and trying to walk down in front of the lava flow to take another GPS coordinate," he said.

During the day, drones mapped fissures and measured dangerous sulfur dioxide emissions, reducing the number of costly helicopter flights needed.

In one daytime mission, emergency personnel received an alert that someone might be in danger in an isolated house. One of CRASAR's drones quickly deployed to verify. Known as "ground-truthing," emergency responders must validate the accuracy of incoming information, especially when it can mean the difference between life and death.

"Citizens were calling in reports, so first responders called CRASAR and we had a strike team that would go and do validation of air quality, lava flow, or lava extent," Adams said. "We acted as an on-demand task force crew."

Expertise, experience, and technology

Many factors contributed to the effectiveness of CRASAR's efforts during the emergency response. Three stand out: technical and scientific expertise, disaster training and experience, and specialized software.

The CRASAR team members' expertise fostered good communication with other first responders and the USGS. Their scientific

The CRASAR team used a thermal sensor to map the lava fronts, cutting through the smoke to show the lava extent.

backgrounds allowed them to speak the same language as the scientists and engineers involved.

Experience with previous disasters prepared the CRASAR team for Kīlauea. They knew which questions to ask in an emergency and what their drones could do to assist the operation.

Finally, they used specialized software to automatically tag images with their locations. They visualized the information in real time on a digital map by using geographic information system (GIS) technology. They employed another application to take panoramic aerial photos automatically instead of manually, expediting situational awareness.

"CRASAR has equipment and technology that was placed above what we're used to," said Christian Wong, executive director, Hawai'i Science and Technology Museum. "In particular, their capability to do 360-degree views of an area very quickly. They used a lot of pre-programmed applications with their drones that are able to do certain tasks that normally, if you relied on a pilot, might take a little while to get done and it wouldn't be as efficient."

Next steps for Kīlauea drone response

The CRASAR team's work was a success. They reduced cost and risk, and increased situational awareness for all involved responders, government agencies, and the public. The team hopes this will build support for future use of robots in disaster response and public safety.

After CRASAR completed its official operations in Hawai'i, the team remained on standby, communicating with first responders often and remaining ready to deploy again if the situation changed.

The work of drones at Kīlauea continued with the University of Hawai'i at Hilo performing daily monitoring of the eruption, as reported by CNN. The drones provided a reliable stream of visual information, helpful in communication with the public during this kind of emergency.

"The visual data drones collect is very useful in helping show the people why they've been evacuated from certain areas," Wong said. "Once they see the devastation and damage, they understand why they cannot be let back to their homes."

Wong noted that CRASAR's participation had an unexpected outcome. It inspired local students from Hawai'i's Big Island to start creating their own disaster robot designed specifically for volcano response.

While the Hawaiian people feel Pele will always be unpredictable—taking and giving land according to natural cycles—emergency responders and scientists can now fly drones above a volcanic eruption for a safer way to observe and measure its awe-inspiring power.

This story by Ryan Lanclos originally appeared as "Hawaii Volcano: Scientists, Emergency Responders Put Drones to Work" on the Esri Blog on August 8, 2018. All images courtesy of Center for Robot-Assisted Search and Rescue unless otherwise noted.

EXTENDING GIS IN THE FIELD FOR RESOURCE ADVISING

Resource Advisors

DURING WILDFIRES AND OTHER EMERGENCY INCIDENTS, emergency responders, public safety officers, and others work tirelessly to protect life and property. Perhaps lesser known is that a host of other professionals often partner with emergency responders to advise them on how to protect at-risk cultural and natural resources. Resource Advisors (READs) can be biologists, hydrologists, archaeologists, tribal liaisons, or specialists from other disciplines who, during an incident, focus on minimizing the impact of disaster response and recovery operations on ecosystems, archaeological sites, and protected species.

More than 80 READs worked on the Ferguson Fire that burned almost 97,000 acres in California in July and August 2018. As the fire spread across the Sierra and Stanislaus National Forests, Yosemite National Park, the homelands of five Native American tribes, and swaths of private land, READs located sensitive resources and developed measures to protect them. Throughout all phases of the fire, they used ArcGIS Collector to streamline their work and ensure that various teams had access to the most up-to-date and relevant information.

The authors of this case study worked together as a GIS specialist and a READ during the suppression repair phase—when the Ferguson Fire was contained but many miles of dozer and hand line, plus hundreds of impacted sites, still needed to be repaired. While GIS has been used in fire operations for decades now, things were different in this fire. The recent adoption of Collector and ArcGIS Online transformed what was once a cumbersome process into a near real-time GIS operation.

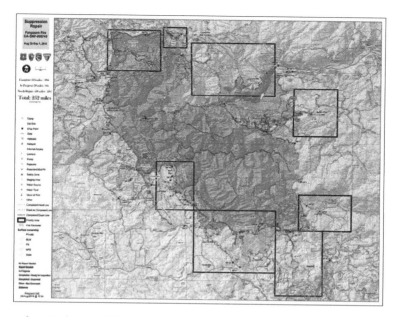

Before the fire was fully contained, Resource Advisors (READs) and GIS specialists worked together to start mapping what needed to be done during the suppression repair phase. Map created by Elizabeth Hale, National Park Service.

From hand-marked paper maps to digital dexterity

During a fire, READs go into the field alongside fire crews to recommend and help implement measures to safeguard cultural and natural resources. In a typical day, READs can be seen protecting a sensitive archaeological site from being destroyed by equipment or saving historic buildings by wrapping them with fire-resistant foil. They recommend where to use lower-impact hand crews rather than heavy equipment. And after the fire has been contained, they help develop repair plans that specify how to restore slopes to limit erosion, where to disperse vegetation to benefit wildlife, and more.

To do all this, they rely on the same maps and GIS data that fire crews use, and then some. While READs are keeping track of fire operations, they also check up on sensitive sites and map areas that need to be repaired. Before they had Collector, they did this with a mix of paper maps, GeoPDFs, and handheld GPS devices. Each night, READs delivered their updates—often a combination of GPS files and paper maps marked with different-colored highlighters—to a GIS specialist, who would digitize the new information and print out maps for READs to mark up by hand the following day.

During the Ferguson Fire, however, the lead READs saw an opportunity to expand the use of mobile GIS. They brought on GIS specialists to support the READ team directly. For the first time, all READs had access to a frequently updated map in Collector, rather than a standard poster-sized paper map. This gave them attribute information and better feature clarity than they had before. They could turn various layers on and off to focus on specific aspects or areas of the wildfire. And because everyone was using a common data platform, READs could more easily communicate with incident managers, agency land managers, and public information officers about the status of sensitive habitats, historic sites, and other important resources that were scattered across a large and complex landscape.

It was a big shift—one that had distinct implications in our different yet intertwined roles as GIS specialist and READ. Here, we offer a closer look at what this digital transformation meant for repairing sensitive areas after the Ferguson Fire.

Supporting GIS in the field

Elizabeth Hale, GIS coordinator, Yosemite National Park

Using Collector and ArcGIS Online during the Ferguson Fire moved incident GIS staff, like myself, away from "let me map that for you" to "see for yourself." With READs able to edit data themselves and sync their updates directly from Collector to the National Incident

Elizabeth Hale.

Feature Service (NIFS), I spent little time digitizing data and down-loading GPS files.

That's not to say there weren't growing pains. Since I no longer facilitated data transactions, data quality assurance had to be managed on new fronts. I had to establish deadlines for syncing edits and make sure READs were not editing the same feature offline. Issues arose with duplicate lines in NIFS, so I had to track down the lines that had accurate attributes. Also, I ended up reviewing the edits and new records for each day's field efforts after they were incorporated into NIFS rather than before.

Overall, though, I really saw this transition enhance communication. Once a wildfire is contained and crews transition to suppression repair, incident GIS staff know that the incident planning team will start asking for daily updates on repairs: What is the status of all the dozer and hand lines? What about the roads that served as fire lines? How many miles have been repaired, and how many still need to be taken care of? We usually write the answers to these questions on a whiteboard in the GIS tent or trailer so the situation leader, plans chief, or lead READ can see them when they pop in.

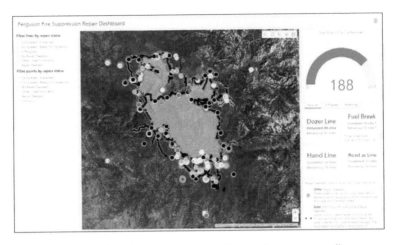

GIS specialist Elizabeth Hale created a dashboard that automatically summarized how many miles of fire line had been repaired, were in progress, or still needed attention.

On the Ferguson Fire, I did something different. I built a dashboard with ArcGIS Dashboards to report the status of suppression repair. I figured it would save me the time and effort it took to recalculate the numbers each morning from a series of queries and selections in the attribute table. The dashboard automatically summarized how many miles had been completed, were in progress, or still needed repair. I broke this up based on fire line type as well. This took reporting to the next level because not only did the dashboard display concrete numbers, but it also allowed incident managers to filter the map layers by repair status to see, on a web map, where specialized equipment or repairs were still needed.

I ended up demonstrating the product to the lead READs and agency administrators from the US Forest Service and the National Park Service. This initiated a productive dialog about how much more GIS could do to support incident response and recovery.

Using GIS in the field

Michelle Barry, conservation planner, US Fish and Wildlife Service, Pacific Southwest Region

As a planner for national wildlife refuges with the US Fish and Wildlife Service, I am occasionally asked to work as a READ for fires or other emergency responses. During the Ferguson Fire, I provided coordination and leadership for more than 30 other READs. It was a challenging assignment involving a large fire area, a sizable READ team, and several agency land managers.

It was clear to me from the beginning that GIS was being used heavily for resource advising during the Ferguson Fire. Upon arrival at the incident command post, my first instructions were to visit the GIS trailer, create a user name in the National Interagency Fire Center's (NIFC) ArcGIS Online organizational account, and download Collector on my smartphone. Soon, I learned how to access geospatial information for the entire expanse of the fire, make notes directly in Collector while out in the field, and later sync any information I gathered so the GIS specialist could incorporate it into the incident map.

As a first-time user, I found Collector to be nimble and user-friendly. It was also very useful for coordinating the READ team. Because the fire spanned such a large geographic area, some READs were stationed hours away from the incident command post. Knowing that they would all sync their updates with ArcGIS Online each night ensured that the NIFS was current across the entire fire area. Thus, when I was asked by agency land managers or others for information on specific sites, I had almost all the data from the READ team at my fingertips. I could tell them how much repair work was still needed in certain areas or how much time it would take for heavy equipment to complete repair work in particular locations.

Michelle Barry.

At some point while working the fire, I remembered being introduced to GIS by my late dad, Mike da Luz. As a wildland fire hotshot, a district ranger, and a regional branch chief of fire and aviation (among other roles at the US Forest Service and, later, Esri), he understood early on how geospatial analysis could better inform land management decisions. More than 25 years ago, he showed me a simple GIS map of forest conditions on the (former) US Forest Service Alsea Ranger District, which encompasses parts of the Siuslaw National Forest in Oregon. As he printed the map, we watched together while four primary-color markers rendered rudimentary symbology on plotter-sized paper. I recall him saying, "GIS will play an important role in natural resource management in the future." It was obvious then that GIS was a valuable tool, but at the time it was also cumbersome and time-consuming.

Now, I can access far more geospatial data on my phone than ever could have been plotted on that piece of paper. My dad had been right: GIS is playing an increasingly integral role in informing resource management. He would have been delighted to see the advancement of GIS in complex fire management scenarios, as exemplified by the Ferguson Fire.

GIS and the future of incident management

GIS has advanced exponentially over the last 25 years. As we continue to look forward, it will be exciting to see what geospatial analysis can bring to future resource management in general—and to fire incident management specifically.

This story by Michelle Barry and Elizabeth Hale originally appeared as "How the Ferguson Fire Extended GIS in the Field for Resource Advising" in the Spring 2019 issue of *ArcNews*. All images courtesy of National Park Service and US Fish and Wildlife Service unless otherwise noted.

GETTING STARTED WITH GIS

G IS MAPS AND ANALYTICS OFFER REAL-TIME SITUATIONAL awareness of resource locations and operational effectiveness during an emergency. Maps, dashboards, and story maps improve communication with the public and media. Next are some recommended steps to help you be better prepared. You can find links to the resources mentioned in this section on the book web page at **go.esri.com/dwd-resources.**

Share public information maps

Public information maps report the status of active incidents, show areas affected by incidents, and alert people to changing conditions. Here are some noteworthy examples:

- Coronavirus COVID-19 Global Cases Dashboard

- Earthquake public information map

- Flooding public information map

- Hurricane public information map

- Severe weather public information map

- Wildfire public information map

Ensure that maps are ready to go "viral" and are following best practices for highly scalable ArcGIS Online web applications using this blog: *Essential Configurations for Highly Scalable (Viral) ArcGIS Online Web Applications.*

Create real-time dashboards

Real-time GIS dashboards support decision makers and responders during emergencies. Dashboards are also an efficient and effective way to keep the public, media, and local and national leadership apprised of current and changing conditions:

- **Bushfires in Victoria:** This dashboard helped track the extent and severity of bushfires in the state of Victoria, Australia, during the 2019-2020 season.

- **COVID-19 pandemic dashboards:** A large number of dashboards were created to provide situational awareness of the COVID-19 outbreak. This dashboard, created by the Johns Hopkins University Center for Systems Science and Engineering, has been viewed hundreds of millions of times by people around the world.

- **Puerto Rico earthquake response dashboards:** To help with emergency response efforts, the US Federal Emergency Management Agency (FEMA) created several dashboards to help with its operations in Puerto Rico in early 2020, such as this one for damage assessment.

- **Floodgate monitoring dashboard:** The Emergency Spatial Support Center (ESSC), a branch of Esri Indonesia, created a dashboard to help monitor floodgates in the city of Jakarta, Indonesia, during a severe flooding event in January 2020.

- **Deploy damage assessment apps:** Damage assessment apps allow you to deploy teams in the field as quickly as possible to assess and determine where and when to deploy recovery resources as well as to support the disaster declaration process. See how to deploy ArcGIS Survey123 as well as new tips and tricks that can help you in the field.

Learn by doing

Hands-on learning will strengthen your understanding of GIS and how it can be used to improve disaster response. In this Learn ArcGIS Path, a collection of free story-driven lessons allows you to experience GIS when it is applied to real-life problems. The Learn ArcGIS Path includes many lessons:

- **Monitor real-time emergencies:** Keep track of fast-changing situations with ArcGIS Dashboards.

- **Find potential hurricane shelters:** Locate potential hurricane shelter sites in the city of Houston.

- **Analyze COVID-19 risk using ArcGIS Pro:** Create risk maps for transmission, susceptibility, resource scarcity, and risk profiles for targeting intervention areas.

Get there faster with GIS templates

Esri's disaster response templates quickly address the short-term impacts of an incident, maintain situational awareness, conduct initial damage assessments, and inform key stakeholders and the public. Here is a partial list of the templates for quickly creating maps and apps:

- **Maintain situational awareness:** Emergency management staff can use this collection of maps and apps to understand an incident or event, allocate response resources, and communicate status.

- **Produce emergency maps:** Emergency management maps can be used by mapping technicians to create a standard set of briefing and response maps.

- **Assess damage:** Damage assessment apps can be used by field inspectors to conduct structural damage assessments in a connected or disconnected environment.

- **Brief key stakeholders:** Incident briefing maps can be used by emergency management personnel to brief key stakeholders during an incident or event.

- **Communicate road closures:** This map can be used by emergency management staff to maintain an inventory of road closures and communicate closures and detours to travelers.

- **Allocate response resources:** Emergency management personnel can use this map to plan logistical operations and manage resource requests during an incident or event.

You can browse all solution templates on the book web page at **go.esri.com/dwd-resources.**

Ask for help

Esri's Disaster Response Program (DRP) has provided GIS support to Esri users and the global community during disasters and crises of all types and sizes for more than 25 years. The DRP can provide data, software, configurable applications, and technical support for emergency GIS operations. Here's how Esri's Disaster Response Program can help:

- **ArcGIS software:** Existing Esri customers can temporarily extend existing licenses to support their organization's increased GIS requirements during a disaster response. If you're new to GIS or not yet a customer, you can gain temporary access to GIS software through the program.

- **Workflow implementation:** Esri can implement or help you configure solutions to support situational awareness, impact analysis, damage assessment, operational briefings, or public information during your response.

- **Data:** Put your response in context by using existing data from ArcGIS Online and ArcGIS Living Atlas of the World, such as real-time weather, traffic, hazards, infrastructure, and demographics. The DRP can connect you with incident-specific data shared by the response community and the private sector.

- **Technical support:** During your response, gain access to premium support services to address any question or issue related to ArcGIS.

- **Maps for the media:** Request embedded maps or interview topic experts for your disaster-related editorial features and news stories.

If you need emergency GIS help for your current disaster response, please request assistance from Esri's Disaster Response Program.

For additional resources and links to live examples, visit the book web page at **go.esri.com/dwd-resources.**

PART 3

DISASTER RECOVERY

EMERGENCY MANAGEMENT PROFESSIONALS NEED TOOLS that help prioritize recovery actions and ensure that emergency management recovery dollars make a difference. GIS maps and analytics help document and manage the process of debris removal, plan and distribute resources where the community needs them most, and monitor and evaluate recovery indicators while providing operational transparency to the public about recovery efforts and spending.

Ensure survivors get the help they need

Understand where recovery efforts are most needed and ensure the public knows where to go for recovery assistance. GIS maps identify ongoing community recovery efforts, the planned location of disaster recovery projects, and where survivors can find resources.

Clean up the community

Document the amount and type of debris, and assign and manage the removal process. Supervise and report on cleanup status to ensure debris removal contracts are fulfilled.

Monitor and evaluate recovery efforts

Engage the community in recovery initiatives with interactive maps. Communicate progress, demonstrate accountability, and show that recovery efforts are open to review.

GIS in action

This section looks at real-life stories of how organizations use GIS to help recover from disasters; the section also provides recommended steps for implementing GIS in an organization.

RELIEF WORKERS USE DRONE IMAGERY TO HELP REFUGEES

International Organization for Migration

THE REGION OF BANGLADESH KNOWN AS COX'S BAZAR near the Bay of Bengal seems an unlikely candidate for a spontaneous metropolis. The country has the second-highest rate of disasters in Asia and the Pacific with conditions that include heavy monsoon rains, flooding, and landslides. Because of its coastal location, Cox's Bazar also endures cyclones.

Yet, since 1991, Cox's Bazar has been a refuge for the Rohingya people fleeing neighboring Myanmar. As a Muslim minority group in a predominantly Buddhist country, the Rohingya have endured decades of ethnic and religious persecution.

In August 2017, Burmese security forces launched massive attacks on predominantly Rohingya areas of Myanmar. In one of the largest forced migrations in modern history, hundreds of thousands of Rohingya left their homes on foot and crossed the border to Bangladesh. Many made their way to the Kutupalong Balukhali camp.

Prior to the influx, Kutupalong Balukhali and camps in Teknaf housed around 200,000 people. Within weeks, the population ballooned to 500,000. It quickly became one of the world's most densely packed refugee camps in a resource-scarce country that already has some of the world's densest living conditions.

The population increase created enormous logistical challenges for the International Organization for Migration (IOM), which works with the Bangladeshi government and the United Nations High Commissioner for Refugees (UNHCR) to administer the camps. In particular, IOM staff are challenged in the region's rainy season that spans from June through September. Nearly one-third

Charging the drone battery, preparing the flight plan, and running through a checklist precede every mapping flight.

of the camp—including one-quarter of its latrines and nearly half of its hand pumps for water—is at risk for flooding and landslides. Heavier rainfall also correlates with increased health risks.

Using drones to map the unmappable

The overarching need for workers at IOM and in the Bangladeshi government was to visualize the camp's extent. Getting a sense of how—and how many—people were transforming Kutupalong could help answer questions about how to accommodate them. City planners require maps with detailed information about land, population, and infrastructure. The new Kutupalong Balukhali was a cartographic blank slate.

"When I was deployed in September (2017), there was no clear visual representation of the extent of the camp," said Sebastian Ancavil, international mission and geographic information system officer at IOM. "We were in the dark, because even a month after the

The drone-derived map of Kutupalong is shared on a big billboard.

exodus, nobody had good information about the situation. That's
why we requested to have a drone fly over it."

Remotely piloted aircraft—commonly known as drones—are
used for many situations that require aerial surveilling, from forest fires to power lines. For the Kutupalong Balukhali project, a
drone alone proved insufficient. Doing the job right would require
additional technology.

Ancavil's professional specialty is GIS software that organizes
geographically specific data onto digital maps. For Ancavil and his
team, a drone with GIS capabilities provided the first comprehensive
view of Kutupalong Balukhali's ongoing transformation.

Before drones became a viable option, Ancavil employed GIS for
similar purposes. After a devastating earthquake hit Haiti in 2010,
he used satellite imagery to monitor rebuilding efforts in Port-au-
Prince. The accelerated pace of this rebuilding meant that the imagery was often outdated before it became available.

Although GIS technology was more limited at that time, Port-au-Prince was an established urban area with preexisting maps that provided a baseline of information to assess earthquake damage. Kutupalong Balukhali presented the opposite challenge, as no maps existed of the quickly created community. Haiti provided the laboratory to create the drone mapping approach. "In Haiti, we went from nothing to something," Ancavil said of the technological innovations to create up-to-date maps. "For Bangladesh, the technology and methodology were there, but there were no existing maps."

Making drones smart

Mapping Kutupalong Balukhali involved a third technology, artificial intelligence (AI), to augment GIS data. The addition of AI gives today's GIS the ability to automatically and quickly process complex imagery. The drone imagery—combined with map data from OpenStreetMap and other partners—could be programmed to recognize and categorize geographic features, including buildings, human-made objects, vegetation, and soil. (To alleviate privacy concerns, the drone is flown at an altitude too high to capture recognizable images of individuals.)

These images give Kutupalong Balukhali camp administrators a comprehensive view of the area's ad hoc structure. Kutupalong Balukhali is subdivided into 23 smaller camps, each containing around 1,500 blocks, with around 100 families per block. Every block has a community leader who represents the block and communicates its needs, including food, education, and security.

This information becomes part of the GIS database, along with a community leader's rough population count, which allows relief workers to visualize the density of a block. "We draw small polygons on the map so that it's easier for a community leader to give information that helps our field team assess the block," Ancavil said.

Use of the drone creates a community event, with young people particularly interested.

Capturing a changing landscape

The combination of drone imagery, GIS, and AI also helps workers understand the land the camp occupies. An influx this large involves massive environmental upheaval. Thousands who fled with nearly nothing were forced to grab bamboo and other materials for shelter, causing deforestation that exacerbates existing environmental challenges. The camp expansion even impacted elephant migration routes, yet another danger camp residents face.

"We can remove all the human construction from the map," Ancavil explained. "Then you're left with just the ground surface, which lets us provide a digital terrain model to partners who calculate landslide risk and flood modeling."

In addition to mapping the camp and helping site planning and development, the use of GIS for Kutupalong Balukhali provides a platform for a broad range of data about people and place pertaining to the camp. With mobile devices, relief workers from UNICEF and other agencies can access various cloud-based datasets. "We are a data provider," Ancavil explained. "We share the information with our partners, through the Humanitarian Data Exchange (HDX) platform, for example, and they can take whatever they need to do their work."

The estimated population of Kutupalong Balukhali and satellite camps that have formed around it, including those in Teknaf, hovered around 900,000 at the beginning of 2020. As ongoing drone flights provide bird's-eye views of the camp, the new data provides ground-level context. The result is a living document that evolves with the camp.

The drone also had the unexpected effect of providing an outlet for childhood fascination. "I had a group of kids follow me on the first mission," Ancavil said. "I didn't understand them, and they didn't understand me, but they stayed with me all day."

This story by Ryan Lanclos originally appeared as "Relief Workers Rely on Drone Imagery to Help Bangladesh Refugee Camp" on the Esri Blog on January 15, 2020. All images courtesy of International Organization for Migration unless otherwise noted.

THE EYE AFTER THE HURRICANE

The National Insurance Crime Bureau and a coalition of geospatial organizations

AFTER THREE CATEGORY 4 HURRICANES STRUCK THE UNITED States in less than a month in 2017—Hurricane Harvey in Texas, Hurricane Irma in Florida, and Hurricane Maria in Puerto Rico and the US Virgin Islands—rescue and recovery workers needed information about the location and extent of impact, fast.

First responders were looking for people injured, trapped, or otherwise in need. Humanitarian organizations needed to deliver food, water, supplies, and medical care to victims. Federal and state agencies were coordinating relief efforts while ensuring safety and figuring out how to restore services. And insurers needed to begin fulfilling claims so people could start rebuilding their homes.

Hurricane Irma's wind and rain pummeled Las Olas Boulevard in Fort Lauderdale, Florida.

With a limited number of first responders in each affected location, everyone involved in the rescue and recovery work relied on eyes in the sky to report what was going on below. For this triple hurricane assault, these eyes came in the form of aerial sensors that produced accurate, detailed imagery so people and organizations could get a quick, up-to-date view of what was happening on land.

To obtain and deliver this imagery, a coalition of leading geospatial firms formed a partnership with the National Insurance Crime Bureau (NICB). Together, they acquired and published high-resolution imagery for nearly 24,000 square miles across Texas, Florida, Puerto Rico, and the US Virgin Islands.

Vexcel Imaging, an Esri partner that provides high-end mapping products and geospatial data services, managed the response, leading the efforts of some of the nation's largest and most advanced aerial mapping companies, including Esri partners such as Quantum Spatial, Sanborn Map Company, GPI Geospatial, and Aerial Surveys. Each of these organizations provided aircraft equipped with Ultra-Cam vertical or oblique aerial sensors to ensure the highest-quality and most accurate imagery possible. Esri served as a member of the coalition, and those involved in response and recovery efforts used an array of ArcGIS software and apps to access, visualize, analyze, and record spatial data.

"The disastrous aftermath of the hurricanes called for the right coalition of organizations to rapidly collect critical information for assessing regional impact and to ultimately help provide relief to those in need," said Erik Jorgensen, Vexcel's president. "Vexcel Imaging is fortunate to have partners in leading aerial mapping companies to rapidly deploy assets to quickly capture aerial imagery of affected areas, and in Esri to make available that critical data in a platform that can be broadly and easily accessed."

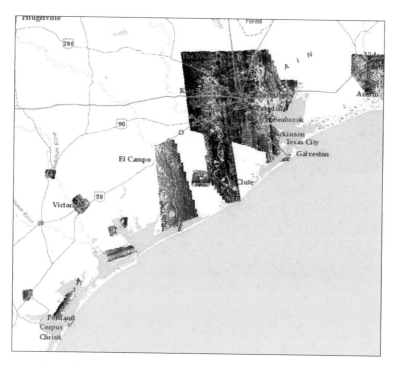

A coalition of leading geospatial firms, led by Vexcel Imaging, acquired and published high-resolution imagery for nearly 24,000 square miles across Texas, Florida, Puerto Rico, and the US Virgin Islands. Imagery courtesy of Vexcel Imaging.

To clearly see what was happening on the ground without having to be physically present in every disaster zone, the coalition collected 3-inch and 6-inch resolution top-down nadir imagery, as well as 45-degree oblique aerial views from the four cardinal directions at 3-inch resolution. The coalition focused its oblique imagery collection on concentrated areas that were directly in the path of each hurricane, as well as on locations that sustained considerable structural damage from winds. For larger areas where massive flooding occurred, the coalition used ultralarge-footprint UltraCam models

With stereo orthoimagery, which is viewed with 3D glasses, users got a better idea of where the storm knocked down trees or winds ripped the roofs off houses. Imagery courtesy of Vexcel Imaging.

to rapidly capture 6-inch nadir imagery. In addition to these aerial views, NICB equipped a vehicle with Vexcel's Mustang mobile mapping sensor system to capture streetside photography.

With this collection of imagery from multiple vantage points, rescue and recovery workers gained a clear view of which buildings had been destroyed, what streets were obstructed by fallen trees and electrical wires, and where the flooding made roads impassable—making it easier for them to get started with their work.

A race against time

Aerial imagery collected in the hours and days that followed Hurricanes Harvey, Irma, and Maria provided the most precise and up-to-date depiction of features and conditions on the ground. It served as a crucial tool in determining how badly wind and flooding had affected coastal communities, major ports, waterways, coastlines, and infrastructure.

"Imagery is integral to disaster response and recovery, as it enables people to accurately determine how a location looked before the event and how it has been affected by the event," said Lawrie Jordan, Esri's director of imagery and remote sensing. "ArcGIS is a comprehensive platform for integrating all forms of imagery into GIS, and it plays a critical role in making such imagery accessible as quickly as possible."

After a storm, it is a race against time to acquire, process, and make hurricane event imagery available to end users. For this series of hurricanes, the coalition collected about 100 terabytes of source data. In traditional mapping workflows, it could take weeks or months to process this data and create a set of orthophoto mosaics to serve as basemaps in various apps. Yet in these cases, as soon as a processing facility received the raw data, Vexcel software transformed it into the individual camera image (the standard output file type for Vexcel Imaging) and directly uploaded it to cloud storage. Simultaneously, Vexcel acquired data from global positioning systems (GPS) and inertial measurement units (IMUs) and processed it to provide georeferencing information about the camera locations.

Additionally, Esri installed ArcGIS Image Server on a set of Amazon Web Services Elastic Compute Cloud instances and configured it to provide the coalition with dynamic image services of all the available imagery. Vexcel and Esri staff used ArcGIS to perform on-the-fly orthorectification based on the best collected orientation data and digital terrain models from the US Geological Survey. The dynamic image services were then added to ArcGIS Online as items, which enabled credentialed users to have automatic access to them in their apps and viewers.

NICB also built a web app using ArcGIS Web AppBuilder that allowed the public to enter an address or point of interest, immediately see imagery from before and after the hurricane, and take measurements—of fallen trees, the extent of flooding, and more—from both nadir and oblique imagery. In addition, the web app permitted first responders, insurance agents, the public, and employees from the Red Cross and the Federal Emergency Management Agency (FEMA) to add layers of public or private data, such as insurance policy information, on top of the imagery. This enabled them to see instantly which properties were damaged and which ones were okay.

Thus, with no time to waste, hurricane response and recovery teams received imagery, information, and insight immediately via web services that connected directly to their desktops and mobile devices.

Keeping imagery current

In the weeks following the hurricanes, the coalition acquired new aftermath imagery each day and added it to the service. Vexcel and Esri refined the aircraft orientation parameters and updated services with new imagery without having to make any changes to the apps, meaning that users continued to have a seamless experience. As people accessed the imagery, ArcGIS Pro and ArcGIS Image Server performed complex, on-the-fly processing so users could retrieve imagery more quickly and optimize the image display for their location. Unlike the traditional approach, in which a user must orthorectify and mosaic all the imagery first, this new process took much less time and did not result in a loss of imagery detail.

Parallel to creating the dynamic image services, processing the imagery in the cloud allowed ArcGIS Pro to create traditional static orthomosaics as tile caches, which were served for public use in ArcGIS Online. For such image processing tasks, ArcGIS immediately delivered the best fit-for-use imagery and then created the georeferenced imagery later.

"A cloud-computing environment using ArcGIS Image Server and ArcGIS Online enabled tremendous scalability in storage and processing power," said Peter Becker, Esri's imagery product manager. "The teams were able to quickly process and deliver a massive amount of imagery and provide quick, easy access to the first views of hurricane destruction."

To further improve image interpretability (the capacity of imagery to depict features such as trees, houses, and roads), Esri provided stereo orthos within the web apps. With the added height perspective, users could see overlapping imagery in stereo, or 3D, and get a better view of where the storm knocked down trees and recreational vehicles or winds ripped the roofs off houses.

The coalition collected nadir imagery to provide rescue and recovery workers with a bird's-eye view of damage from Hurricane Harvey. Imagery courtesy of Vexcel Imaging.

A whole new level for catastrophe response

Furnishing imagery data within a GIS framework is making it easier to retrieve and use vital information for natural disaster rescue and recovery efforts. During Hurricanes Harvey, Irma, and Maria, coalition teams quickly accessed and interpreted imagery by using the internet, cloud computing technology, and ArcGIS.

NICB made available on its website high-resolution aerial images of the areas affected by each of the three hurricanes. Users can search for an individual location in the address bar to view a before-and-after comparison.

"GIS and cloud compute technology takes the industry response to a catastrophe to a whole new level," said NICB president and CEO Joe Wehrle. "We have received overwhelmingly positive feedback from emergency personnel, law enforcement, and our insurance company members in Texas. We believe it is also important to share this with those who have been impacted by the hurricanes."

This story by Jessica Wyland originally appeared as "The Eye After the Hurricane" in the Winter 2018 issue of ArcNews. All images courtesy of the National Insurance Crime Bureau and a coalition of geospatial organizations unless otherwise noted.

AFTER A DISASTER, IMAGERY GIVES INSURANCE COMPANIES A CLEAR PICTURE

Travelers Insurance

SOME OF THE MOST FAMOUS PLANES IN THE WEATHER world are hurricane hunters, piloted by steely nerved aviators who fly into storms to measure what is imperceptible to people on the ground. Since the first storm-chasing pilot plunged into a hurricane on a dare in 1943, the practice has become a standard tool of weather forecasting.

Today, a new breed of flier—with a little less derring-do but an equally important mission—is helping people see what was previously unseen.

Struggling for basic awareness

Human ingenuity can be a poor match for nature's strength. When hurricanes, wildfires, or tornadoes strike, the human instinct is to hunker down or flee. In the aftermath, even our most adaptable tools can fail. All-terrain equipment and amphibious vehicles often can't enter disaster zones when obstacles abound or dangerous conditions persist.

That can leave residents, first responders, and government officials struggling to gain a basic awareness of what has happened and what to do next. Such blind spots slow operations at a time when delays can be measured in lives lost.

Eager to overcome those limitations, a consortium of insurance companies worked to change the nature of recovery. They formed the National Insurance Crime Bureau's Geospatial Intelligence Center (GIC) on the premise that aircraft can help rapidly identify damage

Aerial photographs show the same house before and after a wildfire.

from large-scale weather events that would otherwise take a long time to discover—essentially uncovering the unseen.

If early results are any indication, this new brand of visibility could soon be as routine as a pilot cutting through the eye of a hurricane.

Operational visibility from the sky

The work of the GIC is possible through a fleet of small airplanes equipped with high-resolution cameras and on-demand computing power and location intelligence technology.

The center's mission is to spot changes on the ground. It sets a baseline by shooting ultra-high-definition aerial photography across the country on an annual schedule. Then, when major weather events hit, pilots begin shooting images of the damage as soon as weather allows.

"One of the powerful uses of this tool is that with the aerial imagery, we can increase our engagement with our customers before our claim professionals have physically deployed into an impacted area," says Don Florek, vice president of catastrophe management at Travelers Insurance.

Imagery alone doesn't give Travelers and its peers a head start on customer care; it yields data but not necessarily context. To see what people on the ground can't see, Travelers imports the aerial photographs into a GIS and melds the raw imagery with road networks, clients' addresses, and weather data.

Since most weather events cover many square miles, company analysts created an artificial intelligence (AI) model that speeds up the identification process. Trained on thousands of images and powered by machine learning, the program quickly flags locations where clients have been affected.

Florek describes the location intelligence that Travelers sees with the resulting GIS-based smart maps. "We aggregate millions of data points from weather services to create event overlays, allowing us to visualize the data. The sophisticated use of layered geospatial insights enhances our overall operational intelligence," he explained.

That data could include wind speeds, rainfall—even the diameter of hail that fell in a particular location. Operational awareness of this kind gives Travelers and its clients two advantages: vision and speed.

Reaching out without prompt

Some Travelers clients initiate claims soon after an adverse event. Others can't access their neighborhoods to see what has happened to their homes. In those cases, Travelers can now use its view of the unseen to initiate contact. This happened in the days after the Camp Fire decimated Paradise, California, in 2018.

"We used the aerial imagery and the geospatial applications to assess property damage throughout the evacuated areas, allowing us to identify homes that had been completely destroyed or even partially damaged," Florek said. The imagery "allowed us the information to begin reaching out to those customers to identify if they were safe [and] to begin the claim process and begin to understand how best we could help them. That's completely different than how we would've approached something several years ago, without having that same level of insight," he noted.

First responders and local officials now enjoy the same increased visibility, since the GIC provides imagery to them as well.

"That bird's-eye view of the affected area gives first responders important clues to where they should deploy resources at a time when speed is critical," said Ryan Bank, managing director of the GIC.

Focusing on customer satisfaction

For now at least, the pilots of twin-engine aircraft and their high-resolution cameras haven't replaced traditional methods of disaster assessment; insurance adjusters still must inspect damage in person to complete most appraisals. But the imagery, combined with location intelligence and AI, bolsters situational awareness immediately after tumultuous events, when speed of recovery is critical.

It is also proving valuable in other areas of the insurance life cycle. Risk analysts, for instance, have begun using location intelligence from imagery to fine-tune models of risk. With GIS-based analysis, they can more accurately predict threats to specific locations. Fraud examiners are interested in aerial imagery, too, since it creates an additional check on homeowners who falsely claim that a weather event damaged their property.

In claims handling, the ability to see what was previously unseen has already helped Travelers increase its customer responsiveness. For example, in 2018, Travelers says it resolved 94 percent of claims within 30 days—during a year crowded with major disasters. That type of efficiency is key in the insurance industry, where the second-most common client complaint is that their payments were delayed.

For Florek and the team at Travelers, having eyes in the sky and location intelligence on the ground has helped turn understanding into action.

"The layered geospatial insights really provide us with a whole different level of operational insight to understand the event, the impact for our customers, and how best to deploy the right people to the right place as quickly as possible," Florek says.

This story by Alexander Martonik originally appeared as "The Unseen: After a disaster, imagery gives insurance companies a clear picture" in WhereNext magazine, July 23, 2019. Photo courtesy of Vexcel Imaging.

AUTHORITIES MAP AND MODEL DAMAGE FROM DEADLY ALABAMA TORNADOES

Federal Emergency Management Agency, National Weather Service, and Alabama Law Enforcement Agency

DOZENS OF TORNADOES RIPPED THROUGH SOUTHEASTERN US states the first week of March 2019. Two twisters touched down an hour apart along nearly the same path in Lee County, Alabama, leaving authorities racing to assess damage and search for survivors.

Four days before the deadly storm, forecasters predicted it due to a strong weather pattern known as a shortwave trough. The National Weather Service's Storm Prediction Center issued a Particularly Dangerous Situation tornado watch for much of Alabama, northwest Georgia, southeast Mississippi, and southern middle Tennessee. The forecast marked a greater than 95 percent probability of at least two tornadoes and at least one of those being a strong tornado.

In Lee County, the first tornado struck with more than 170 mile-per-hour winds (rated an EF4 on the Enhanced Fujita Scale). Leaving a trail of destruction nearly a mile wide and 24 miles long, the tornado tore down trees, tossed cars, and leveled homes to piles of debris. Twenty-three people lost their lives.

When any disaster strikes, authorities must act quickly to assess damage. In the case of tornadoes, the National Oceanic and Atmospheric Administration's National Weather Service is one of the first on the scene with a damage survey team. The team gathers data to map storm start and end points, path length and width, and wind magnitudes.

"I was initially called by the Alabama Emergency Management Agency to support efforts there," said Jared Bostic, deputy geographic

The EF5 tornado that hit Joplin, Missouri, on May 22, 2011, caused widespread damage, including leveling this school. This event provided the impetus for advancement in disaster recovery assistance.

information officer with the Alabama Law Enforcement Agency. "I took the tornado swaths and then mapped an impact summary, using a geographic information system (GIS) to calculate the population and number of households that could be affected within those swaths, including the number of businesses."

This initial mapping gives first responders crucial information about potential scope and scale of the event and helps the search and rescue effort.

Modeling damage

After a disaster, officials at the Federal Emergency Management Agency (FEMA) need specific details of damage before they can determine the level of federal recovery assistance. Typically, it is up to local authorities to provide information. To reduce that burden, FEMA started working on a partially automated imagery-derived model to conduct preliminary house-by-house damage estimates.

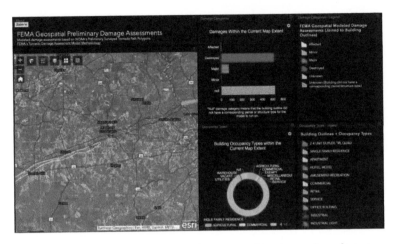

The Federal Emergency Management Agency combined a number of inputs to create this dashboard that tallies the impacts of the tornadoes that hit on March 3, 2019.

"The impetus for this solution goes back to the EF5 tornado that hit Joplin, Missouri, in May of 2011," said Christopher Vaughan, geospatial information officer at FEMA. "When 500 federal employees showed up and began asking for data, it was a struggle for the city's GIS person to come up with what got hit and how bad it got hit."

It took a week to fly updated aerial imagery and conduct house-by-house damage assessments.

"We have significantly improved the time it takes to gain an awareness and understanding of tornado damage," said Vaughan. "We have gone from five to six days down to less than 24 hours."

Vaughan and his team attribute the faster assessment time to a national building footprint and parcel dataset, which allow for quicker calculations of damage to homes and structures. FEMA has been working with the National Geospatial-Intelligence Agency and its contractor, CoreLogic, to develop the national parcel base, building on Microsoft's release of national building outlines. This data combines with Enhanced Fujita wind speed ratings that help to assess the level of damage caused to different structures based on the wind speed.

"The preliminary model takes land use data within the tornado track to estimate the level of damage to individual structures," said Madeline Jones, geophysical data scientist at New Light Technologies, a FEMA contractor. "As soon as we have wind speeds, we can run the model to calculate the estimated level of damage. From there, we can create a spreadsheet, stand up a web application, and create a feature service that others can consume, all within a few hours."

Speedy assessment enhances situational awareness for teams conducting on-the-ground damage analysis as well as crews working to remove debris, reopen roadways, and restore electrical and communications networks. The preliminary damage review also helps support damage declaration decisions for the impacted communities.

"The model provides an estimated overall scoping of the incident size, shape, and extent to support a variety of crisis decisions," Vaughan said. "The faster and more accurate we are, the better the evidence-based decisions. We're always fighting time, and time is life."

Combining many inputs

During every disaster, many people and agencies rally to assist local first responders. In the case of the Alabama tornadoes, the American Red Cross quickly deployed volunteers with a survey-based field application to conduct door-to-door damage assessments. The National Insurance Crime Bureau's Geospatial Intelligence Center (GIC) collected aerial imagery through a partnership with Vexcel Imaging and Esri and made the imagery available to first responders and insurance company members.

With today's modern geospatial infrastructure, data from multiple organizations can be securely shared as web services. This includes web services for aerial imagery, field-collected data, basemaps, and more. Together, this data can be combined in purpose-built applications that visually communicate different place-based aspects of the operation.

"With the imagery service coming from the GIC, I created a change detection slider for pre- and post-disaster imagery," Bostic said. "You can just move that slider back and forth to see a home before and after the tornado."

Bostic and his team use ArcGIS StoryMaps and ArcGIS Dashboards to communicate information at a glance to decision makers and first responders in the field. These modern apps help fill in data gaps for first responders and operators working to save lives and property during a disaster.

Bostic created a damage assessment dashboard to tally the Red Cross damage appraisals. "Once an assessment is done and submitted in the field," he explained, "it updates the dashboard with the date and time of the most recent submission, the type of home it is, and the extent of structural damage. A ticker tallies the number of assessments to date."

Recurring incidents

Alabama is one of the few places in the world to experience two tornado seasons, adding November and December along with severe spring weather.

"There were 300 tornado touchdown points in the spring of 2011, and it caused chaos," Vaughan said. "If we were to get hit today with that kind of massive event, we have the technology to quickly deliver information and make sure that we're all communicating and collaborating."

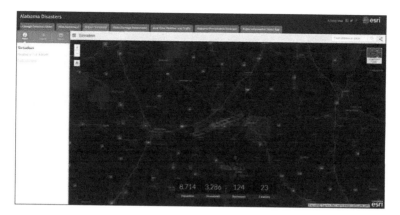

This tabbed map was developed by the Alabama Law Enforcement Agency. This first tab shows tornado paths and tallies the people and businesses impacted.

This tab on the map uses a slider to show before- and after-disaster imagery.

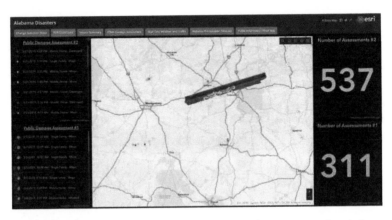

This tab tallied the number of disaster assessments that were completed along the tornado's path.

The quick and impossible-to-predict paths of tornadoes make it one of the more unsettling disasters.

"With hurricanes, you have a week to plan and get people out of harm's way," Bostic said. "We knew we were going to have some bad weather, but you just don't know when and where it's going to drop out of the sky."

Increasing the accuracy of automation

FEMA provides support for all types of disasters. It maintains an online data visualization tool that allows people to review events in each county and state across the United States over time. Records date back to 1953, when federal assistance started.

FEMA's preliminary damage assessment dataset includes close to 1 million records covering all big events, including Hurricane Sandy in 2012 (one of the costliest with $70 billion in damage), the 2013 Moore tornado (most severe winds at 210 mph), the 2011 Joplin tornado (the deadliest since 1947), and more.

"We've made the data publicly available to help with machine learning training," said Vaughan. "Researchers can go back and look at old imagery and use it as training data for algorithms to automate disaster assessments."

FEMA encourages academic use of this data. The goal is to speed the time from when a disaster hits to when it is assessed and communicated to first responders.

This story by Ryan Lanclos originally appeared as "Authorities Map and Model Damage from Deadly Alabama Tornadoes" on the Esri Blog, April 23, 2019. It is the first of a two-part story about damage assessment for the devastating tornadoes in Lee County, Alabama. All images courtesy of Federal Emergency Management Agency, National Weather Service, and Alabama Law Enforcement Agency unless otherwise noted.

MAPPING THE NEEDS OF PEOPLE IMPACTED BY DEADLY TORNADOES

Lee County Emergency Operations Center and the Alabama Fire College

THE SCALE AND SCOPE OF TWO TORNADOES THAT HIT LEE County, Alabama, in early March 2019 surprised many experts. Winds in the first tornado exceeded 170 miles per hour and left a trail of destruction nearly a mile wide and 24 miles long. The second tornado, though less severe, struck along nearly the same path as the first.

"This was the worst damage that I've seen from a tornado," said David Thornburg, section chief, Alabama Fire College. "I saw 24-inch-diameter pine trees snapped 20 feet in the air as well as at the ground, total destruction of mobile homes where the frame rails were left but nothing else was recognizable as a house part, and a house that was picked up and moved 30 to 40 feet onto a road."

Personnel and students from the Alabama Fire College assisted Lee County's Emergency Management Agency to assess damage and address survivor needs.

Ken Busby, the GIS coordinator with Lee County, has firsthand experience understanding the plight of tornado victims.

"I have family who live in Sylvania, Alabama, and their house was completely destroyed [from the tornado that hit Tuscaloosa, Alabama, on April 27, 2011]," Busby said. However, the Lee County event was the worst storm Busby has encountered as a mapping professional.

"My job is to try and get help out to those people, to make sense of the damage, and to support first responders with information and data they need to make decisions," Busby said.

An aerial image taken before the tornado swept through a rural corner of Lee County, Alabama. The red line depicts the center of the tornado's path.

This image illustrates the level of damage caused by the tornado.

A modern combination of field apps and web-based dashboards from Esri aided the county's efforts.

"It put the information in front of the people who needed it and gave them an understanding in great detail of what's happening in the field without having to go out there," Busby said. "They see from the office the full picture of the damage—where it is and where to send people."

Finding those in need

Because of Lee County's rural location, the 2019 storm impacted fewer lives than the Tuscaloosa tornado. But, where the tornadoes hit, they hit hard.

"You can see the power of this type of storm," Busby said. "It's like it came down and just wiped everything off the face of the earth."

Busby equipped firefighters with a survey-based needs assessment app for recording and documenting survivor needs from the community. He routed data coming from the app onto a live dashboard in the Emergency Operations Center (EOC).

"We had a volunteer dedicated to monitoring that information, prioritizing what was immediately needed, and keeping track of less urgent needs like debris cleanup."

Firefighters divided the area on the map into a grid, assigned the work to three divisions, and fanned out with five teams of two people per division.

"Rural folks are used to doing things on their own and often aren't aware of the resources that are available," said Matt Russell, executive director of the Alabama Fire College. "We went door to door to each of the 201 households that were impacted, identifying if they needed volunteers to help clear trees, or if they needed food, water, medicines or personal hygiene items."

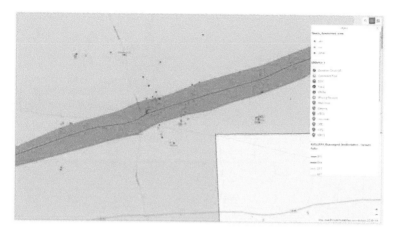

Lee County used a survey-based handheld application to collect the needs of those impacted by the tornado, and aggregated and communicated those needs using this dashboard.

In one instance, firefighters came across a diabetic survivor who needed medicine immediately. Having the real-time link from the field to the EOC meant they could quickly route that request to the Medical Needs section to fill the prescription and get it out to that address quickly.

Sharing perspectives on the damage

An app-based approach also empowers first responders to gather reliable information to share with those impacted, giving them a big-picture understanding of the scale and scope of the event.

"These people are still trying to wrap their head around the fact that they've lost everything," Busby said. "We need to get the information to the people so they can react and get the help they need."

Aerial imagery from airplanes and drones provided a good deal of this information. Lee County had flown aerial imagery for the whole region within the previous year. Along with after-tornado

Mobile homes are notoriously vulnerable in high-wind situations. Here, the wreckage of a home sits wrapped around a tree.

imagery, the before photos provided a good side-by-side comparison of the extent of damage. The National Insurance Crime Bureau's Geospatial Intelligence Center (GIC) collected the first after-tornado aerial imagery in the wake of the event and made that imagery available to first responders.

"The imagery of where the debris scattered helped us guide rescuers where to look," Busby said.

The EOC uses field apps and the dashboard to help manage and coordinate field crews working on the response. From the first responders' perspective, apps fill an information gap and help dispersed teams achieve more together.

"I happen to be on the Alabama Mutual Aid System Advisory Committee, and I'm going to recommend this real-time capability as a primary objective of our search-and-rescue teams," Russell said. "The more information we have upfront, the more efficient and effective we can be in the utilization of our resources."

Though added efficiency is important, speed is not the primary objective.

"We have to make sure we allocate enough time to listen to the people," Russell said. "We need to balance our interests of gathering information versus the mental health needs of victims who want to tell how they survived."

Busby and his team focused on creating a conduit of details for those affected.

"I wanted to be sure I was answering any question I had the power to provide," he said. "That stemmed from my aunts and uncles not having any details at their fingertips when they needed it."

Once the response is over, the long path of recovery and rebuilding begins.

"Recovery is the longest lasting and most intensive activity, including mapping," Busby said. "There's now time to do more analysis and data mining in order to make informed decisions with all the right information in front of us."

This story by Ryan Lanclos originally appeared as "Mapping the Needs of People Impacted by Deadly Tornadoes" on the Esri Blog, April 25, 2019. It is the second of a two-part story about assessing damage from the devastating tornadoes in Lee County, Alabama. All images courtesy of Lee County Emergency Operations Center and the Alabama Fire College unless otherwise noted.

GETTING STARTED WITH GIS

GIS MAPPING AND ANALYTICS ESTABLISHES A COLLABORA-tion pattern across emergency management organizations. Below are some recommended steps to help you be better prepared. You can find links to the resources mentioned in this section on the book web page at **go.esri.com/dwd-resources**.

Create recovery maps

Maps and dashboards show where community recovery efforts are ongoing, where disaster recovery projects are planned, and where survivors can find resources. Here are examples of how GIS maps are used to share disaster recovery efforts with communities:

- Resilient city recovery maps

- Devastation in Nepal: Kathmandu Before and after the April 2015 earthquake

- Katrina +10: A decade of change in New Orleans

- Carr fire imagery

Build a community destination

Provide the community with a single source of information for your recovery efforts. ArcGIS Hub can provide this web destination to share your maps, resources, and initiatives with the community. Here are some noteworthy examples:

- North Carolina COVID-19 rapid recovery for small businesses

- Recovery dashboard—Gallatin, Madison, and Park County areas, Montana

Learn by doing

Hands-on learning will strengthen your understanding of GIS and how it can be used to improve disaster preparedness. In this Learn ArcGIS Path, a collection of free story-driven lessons allows you to experience GIS when it is applied to real-life problems.

Get there faster with GIS templates

Esri's disaster recovery templates help you quickly assess the full impact or extent of an incident, return vital systems to normal operating standards, and execute service and site restoration plans. Here are some of the templates:

- **Identify property damage:** Field inspectors can use this collection of maps and apps to identify property damage and other impacts after an incident or event.

- **Collect safety reports:** Public safety personnel and the general public can use this collection of maps and apps to file health and safety reports important to the community.

- **Manage storm debris:** Collect debris reports made after an incident or event and monitor cleanup activities.

For additional resources and links to live examples, visit the book web page at **go.esri.com/dwd-resources.**

CONTRIBUTORS

Matt Ball
Michelle Barry
JoAnne Castagna
Mike Cox
Dave Fisse
Este Geraghty
Tamara Grant
Elizabeth Hale
Chun-Hung Huang
Lawrie Jordan
Derek Law
Keith Mann
Alexander Martonik
Amen Ra Mashariki
Raj Patil
Monica Pratt
Citabria Stevens
Wen-Ray Su
Jessica Wyland
Chun-Hung Yang